THE SHOTGUN STOCK

THE SHOTGUN STOCK

DESIGN, CONSTRUCTION AND EMBELLISHMENT

Robert Arthur

qTS
535
A73

A69493

South Brunswick and New York: **A. S. Barnes and Company**
London: **Thomas Yoseloff Ltd**

ST. PAUL PUBLIC LIBRARY

© 1971 by A. S. Barnes and Co., Inc.
Library of Congress Catalogue Card Number: 73-107107

A. S. Barnes and Co., Inc.
Cranbury, New Jersey 08512

Thomas Yoseloff Ltd
108 New Bond Street
London W1Y OQX, England

ISBN 0-498-07621-0
Printed in the United States of America

To My Wife
Jane

Contents

9   Acknowledgments

I
11   INTRODUCTION

1
13   About This Book

II
15   THE PARTS OF THE STOCK

2
17   Stock Length
3
21   The Butt
4
27   Pitch
5
30   Cast
6
34   The Grip
7
40   The Fore-end
8
46   The Comb
9
55   Cheekpieces
10
59   The Body of the Stock

The Shotgun Stock

III
SHOTGUN CONTROL AND ACCURACY — 61

11	63	Balance and Recoil
12	69	Special Shotgun Stocks
13	75	Shotgun Sights and Ribs
14	82	The Ballistics of Shotgun Sighting
15	89	Sighting-In the Shotgun

IV
STOCK DESIGN AND FIT — 93

16	95	Shotgun Stock Design
17	105	Fitting the Shotgun Stock
18	115	Experimental Shotgun Stocks

V
THE WOOD — 127

19	129	Gunstock Woods
20	152	Gunstock Finishes
21	156	Checkering and Decoration Of Shotgun Stocks

169   Notes
173   Index

Acknowledgments

The author wishes to express his appreciation to those who have so graciously helped in the preparation of this book.

It certainly would not have been published at all without the encouragement and advice of the benevolent dean of the literature of shooting, Ray Riling. Most of the manuscript was criticized by James C. Hornor, who permitted the author to incorporate something of the classical viewpoint of a rare and accomplished shooting man. Dr. Wayne Murphy, head of the Department of Wood Science and Technology at Pennsylvania State University, scrutinized and made valuable contributions to the chapters on woods and finishes.

Thomas E. Hall of the Winchester Gun Museum, New Haven, Conn. and Harvey Murton of the Arms and Armor Dept. of New York's Metropolitan Museum of Art took the trouble to help the author examine guns in their care. The Manhattan Shirt Co. made their statistics available.

With the exception of the pictures of their try-gun generously furnished by Holland and Holland, Ltd.; all photographs for this book were taken by James F. Gilbert of Chambersburg, Pa.

The author is deeply grateful to those who provided the subject matter, and often their time and facilities, for photography. Commercial establishments include the incomparable Abercrombie and Fitch of New York, the wood importer and stockmaker Flaig's, Millvale, Pa.; Diehl's Sporting Goods, Chambersburg, Pa.; and Walker's, Fort Loudon, Pa. Individuals to be thanked are that remarkable collector of Parker guns Dr. Robert C. Snavely, Mr. George Lyon and the author's shooting companion Thomas C. H. Webster. Special gratitude is due to those who permitted pictures to be taken of the bad as well as the good. Mention in connection with particular photographs has been withheld in any question of quality, or in the case of guns owned by the author.

The author designed and prepared the graphics.

Fort Loudon, Pa.

1
INTRODUCTION

". . . the gun must particularly suit the individual owner; for one gun will no more suit all men, than one coat will fit all wearers; and no man can any more shoot well with a gun that does not come readily to his shoulder and fairly to his eye, then he can be at ease in a coat two sizes under his fit, or walk a foot-race in boots that pinch him."

Frank Forester (H. W. Herbert)[1]

1
About This Book

The literature of the shotgun has concentrated on the mechanical aspects of the gun, on its ballistics, and on the art of shooting. This is the first book about the shotgun stock. It is a what, why, and how-to book written from the American shooter's viewpoint. The considerable body of information that does exist about the stock has been scattered piecemeal in books and articles. One purpose of this book is to collect and present this material in one place. Extensive references are included to provide the reader access to original sources or to more technical data.

The book is intended to be read as a sequence because all of the data about a subject could not be adequately presented in one place without confusion or duplication. The first chapters describe the parts of the stock and attempt to make sense out of traditional or contradictory views about their design and fit. The next chapters provide ballistic and mechanical information that applies to shotgun sighting and fitting. The following chapters offer a method of shotgun stock design and fitting that the author hopes will be of practical value to American shotgunners. The last part of the book is devoted to the technology of gunstock woods and finishes and to gunstock decoration.

Unless otherwise stipulated in the text, the shotgun, of whatever mechanical design, is for field shooting, comparable to the British "game gun," and not one especially intended and stocked for clay pigeon games.

II
THE PARTS OF THE STOCK

2
Stock Length

Gunstock length (*length of pull*) is defined and measured as the distance from the center of the (front) trigger to the center of the butt.

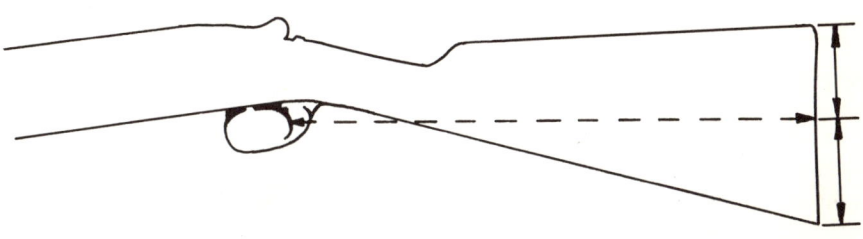

A consideration of the factors involved in the choice of stock length furnishes a good introduction to the state of knowledge about the shotgun stock. Practices and opinions and the reasons given for them are not unanimously accepted.

Factory stock lengths for most 12 gauge field guns offered in the United States at the time of writing (1968) were 13½" (2), 13¾" (2), 14" (29), 14⅛" (1), 14¼" (6), 14⅜" (1), and 14½" (1). This commercial consensus for 14-inch stock length is actually more striking than it seems, for this length is employed by all the principal American manufacturers except Browning (14¼").

Willi Barthold's textbook, which may be taken to represent current German opinion, recommends a 14-inch pull.[2] British practice has been and is to use somewhat longer stocks. Of ten Manton guns made in London early in the nineteenth century measured by the author, seven had stocks between 14½ and 14¾ inches long.[3] Present-day stocks manufactured in or expressly for sale in Britain are typified by Webley's 14⅝" and the AYA "English Range" at 14¾". These lengths correspond to those specified in catalogs describing individually fitted second-hand English "best" guns.

Their national preference for stocks longer than those commercially offered in the United States should lay to rest any rigid ideas about average or standard stock measurements when it is recalled that the British take the shotgun seriously enough to have made stock-fitting a profession. Why the British prefer a longer stock is worth considering. The idea that the use of the longer stock is connected with their present custom of shooting driven (incoming) game must be rejected because the Manton guns mentioned above were stocked before the era of this form of sport. Moreover, American sportsmen experienced in shooting both driven game and game got up over dogs do not believe that different lengths are required for these different types of shooting. The shorter American stock may be related to the popularity of the single trigger here. Nichols pointed out that the long stock gets ¾" shorter when the hand is shifted back to pull the rear trigger, which coincides with the general use of double triggers in England.[4] A different answer may simply be that English game shooters, along with many American trap shooters, are convinced as a matter of experience that longer stocks can be pointed more accurately. The British attitude is all the more interesting because driven game shooting requires fast gun mounting while our trap-shooting rules permit the competitor to mount his gun before he calls for the target.

All authorities emphasize the importance of fitting stock length to the individual. We can start by reviewing their comments on the relationship between stock length and physique. Most agree that physical characteristics such as greater or lesser height, breadth of shoulder, neck length, or arm length call for longer or shorter gun stocks. One English and one American writer have literally prescribed scales of stock length directly proportionate to the shooter's height. Burrard's English scale runs from 14½ to 14¾ inches for heights varying from 5'4" to 6', with provisions for shorter or longer stocks for men on either side of these limits.[5] Askins's American scale specifies a 13½ inch stock for a man of 5'4" up to 14¾ inches for a man 6'4" tall.[6] However, two experienced professional fitters, Robert Churchill[7] and Fred Etchen[8] are sceptical of any simplistic concept of the relation of physique alone to gun fit, including fit for stock length. Neither this Englishman nor this American believes that stockfitting can be done by a rigid formula that prescribes the same stock for two men of the same build. Both would set out to fit two identically built shooters as individuals, with some expectation that each might be best fitted with stocks of different dimensions.

Stock Length

Unlike height, no authority emphasizes arm length alone, perhaps because variations in arm length are compensated for naturally by flexing the arms at the elbow during gun mounting. At any rate, statistics of the Manhattan Shirt Co. show that extremes of arm length are not common.[9] Only ten percent of men wear sleeves shorter than 31 inches or longer than 33 inches. Modern English and American writers believe that there is no message about stock length in the distance between the crook of the trigger finger and the crook of the elbow, although this fancy still enjoys some currency on the continent. From a practical standpoint a stock should be at least long enough to keep the shooter from banging his nose against his thumb or fingertips during recoil. Etchen accordingly invites the shooter to test fit for length by measuring the distance between the nearest digits of the hand holding the grip and the tip of his nose.[10] He believes that the correct interval should be between 1 and 1½ inches.

Psychological factors affecting stock length are claimed by several authors. Churchill postulates that heavier guns need shorter stocks because he believes the shooter pulls the heavier gun toward himself but extends his arms away from himself when holding the lighter one.[11] Several manufacturers who equip heavy magnums with shorter stocks, or lighter guns with longer stocks may subscribe to this theory. This same idea probably underlies Churchill's proposition that as a shooter grows older he will be more comfortable with a shorter stock, presumably because a gun of a given weight will seem heavier to the older shooter.[12] Whelen calls attention to the experience of some shooters who feel that sensible recoil increases with shorter stocks.[13] Burrard advocates longer stocks for longer barreled guns in the interest of gun balance.[14] Without a wink this same author goes on to recommend long-barreled (ergo, long-stocked) guns for tall men because they look in scale, as a tailor might suggest a double-breasted suit. For field shooting fast gun-mounting is the most important factor governing stock length. Fred Etchen flatly stated that he rarely found a stock that was too short, especially for field and skeet shooting.[15] Perhaps the last word should be given to Arthur Hearn who, after a lifetime of stock fitting and coaching, pronounced that there was no such thing as normal stock length.[16]

Many of the elements of stock fit are interdependent. In the present context extremes of pitch can, in effect, change stock length. Because of this interrelationship, pitch and length should be fitted at the same time. Clothing worn is another factor to consider. Most American shooters live in a changeable climate where the thickness of clothing comfortable from the beginning to the end of the hunting season can vary considerably. Stock length should be set so that the gun fits with whatever clothing is to be worn with it. Some writers recommend the use of a removable sleeve type recoil pad to adjust stock length.

A neglected aspect of fit for length is the special importance of correct stock length to young shooters. Many eager boys and girls who might be taught to shoot by competent instructors have been put off for years or forever by a gun that was simply too long in the stock for them to handle. While manufacturers have solicitously offered .22 caliber rifles tailored to the youngster, no one seems to have had the sense to offer an open-choked, balanced, inexpensive shotgun stocked to fit young beginners. Better still, since no one stock length can continue to fit a growing child, a buttplate of the type that is adjustable for length (and height) might well be provided by manufacturers or parents.

In the face of so much advice, the mature shooter who wants to find the best stock length for himself is in about the same position as a boy being taught to shoot by several well-meaning adults all at the same time. If he is a bright, practical youngster he will eventually decide to make up his own mind. Translated into terms of gun-fitting this means that he will accept advice when he can prove it works for him. There is no substitute for simple trial and error until the individual shooter finds the right stock length for himself for a particular gun used for a particular kind of shooting. This general caution will be seen to apply in some degree to the fit of many other parts of the stock.

3
The Butt

The entire flattened end of the gunstock nearest the shooter is called the *butt*. Its upper angle is designated the *heel* (English: *bump*) its lower angle the *toe*. The measured midpoint between the two is called the center of the butt.

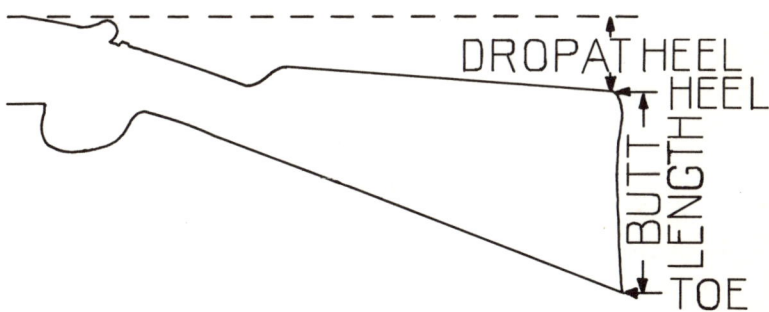

The heel-to-toe length of the butt of American commercial stocks averages about 5¼ inches. Adequate butt length should permit the stock to protrude about one inch or so above and below the points where it comes in actual contact with the shooter's shoulder. Only about two thirds or less of its length is in touch with the soft tissue of the shoulder notch when the gun is held for horizontal or slightly elevated shots, while only a very short length of the butt brings nearly all the force of recoil into contact with the collarbone when the gun is in position for overhead shots.
Shooters with exceptionally muscular or slight shoulders may be suited by a longer or shorter butt. The shooter in doubt about proper length, can check it by placing a ruler in his shoulder notch with the zero at the correct level for the heel and measuring the distance down to a point sufficiently below the bottom edge of the (pectoral)

21

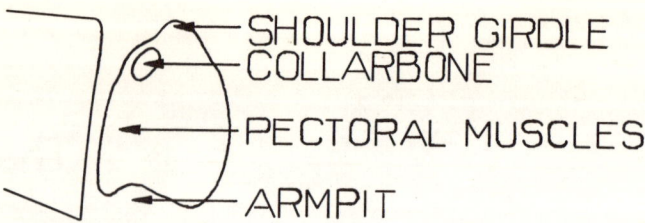

muscles which connect the upper part of the chest with the upper part of the arm. The correct position of the heel when the gun is mounted should be about on a level with the top of the shoulder girdle muscles above and behind the collarbone.

The position of the heel of the butt relative to the rest of the gun is called *drop-at-heel* (English: *bend-at-heel* or *bend*). A stock is said to be straight as it has less drop-at-heel, or crooked as it has more. Drop-at-heel is measured as the vertical distance between the heel and a backward projection of the topline of the barrel(s) or rib. This projection and that for measuring drop-at-comb should be in line with the base of the front sight, not its top. Older guns with hollow and/or swamped ribs can be correctly measured with a straight edge in the low point of the hollow and long enough to avoid error due to the longitudinal concavity of the swamp. Measurement can usually be performed when the gun is placed upside down on a level surface. The average commercial American and German drop-at-heel today is about 2½ inches. The British use about ¼" to ½" less.

Correct drop-at-heel can be defined for an individual shooter only in relation to fit at comb. If fitting were to be started with the comb, and a change in drop-at-heel were made later, the gun's point of impact might be altered so that the comb would not fit, as will be discussed in conjunction with recoil. Thus the butt should be fitted before the comb. A butt that extends a little farther above shoulder level than necessary may help the gun stay on the shoulder as it is rotated upward during direct overhead shooting. If the heel of the butt were set still higher, by using a drop-at-heel even less than the British two inches, as seen in some trap guns, the added height might cause the field shooter to hit himself on the face with the butt when he mounts his gun quickly (Fig. 9, Top). The minimum drop-at-heel for safe (in this respect) gun mounting, regardless of the design of the comb itself, seems to be about 2 inches.

The butt is the agent of recoil contact between the gun and the shooter's shoulder. Most writers endorse the idea that the shooter's perception of a given amount of recoil increases with increasing drop-at-heel. This phenomenon, frequently mentioned in connec-

The Butt

tion with older American stocking styles that employed drop-at-heel as great as 3-3½ inches, can be verified today by comparing the recoil effect when shooting the upper and lower barrels of over-and-under guns. The explanation usually offered, that more discomfort is felt because the gun tends to rotate up more during recoil when the stock has more drop-at-heel, fits the concept of jump discussed in the chapter on recoil.

The intensity of recoil impact can be diminished by spreading it over a larger surface area. While the contribution that can be made to surface area by butt length is limited by the length of the individual's shoulder notch, the butt's surface area can be considerably enlarged by simply making it wider, particularly its lower part. The shooter should therefore use as wide a butt as is comfortable and easy to mount. The surface area of the recoil absorbing part of the butt is greater in the blunt-toed types closer in design to those in fashion in flintlock days (Fig. 1, Lower Left). American commercial hard buttplates are available in unfinished widths from about 1⅜ to 1¾ inches, while recoil pads are available in widths up to 2 inches.

Some modern butts furnished with a narrow pointed toe not only offer less surface area to absorb recoil but may cause a painful bruise if the gun is not perfectly mounted (Fig. 2, Left). Considerable cross-sectional convexity along with rounding of the edges will help make a butt more comfortable (Fig. 2, Right). Flat butts with sharp angles at the sides will cause recoil bruises more easily. The proper butt width for the individual should be determined by trial and error after the butt has been measured and correctly set for cast-at-toe.

Most American shotguns are furnished with butts that are concave lengthwise. This hollow from just below the heel on down to the toe is intended to facilitate positioning of the gun at a consistent level in the shoulder notch. A certain amount of this is probably desirable even in field stocks, but a markedly hollowed heel-to-toe line fits too precisely for quick gun mounting (Fig. 9, Top). The nearly straight line used in many British stocks offers no help in accurate shouldering and requires careful fitting of pitch to avoid reducing the recoil absorbing surface. Butts having a long pointed toe tend to catch on the clothing during mounting. Some buttplate and recoil pad designs shorten the toe by recurving forward below the point of contact with the shoulder (Fig. 9, Top). Greener noted that Capt. Bogardus's famous rival, Dr. Carver, ordered his gun butts chamfered (slightly beveled as seen from above) so that the butt would slope in conformity with the shooter's shoulder notch.[17] Chamfering may contribute to gun fit at the butt for anyone with a marked barrel-chest or unusual shoulder contour.

24   The Shotgun Stock

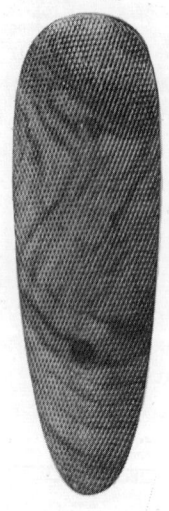 

Fig. 1
Top, Although undeniably handsome, the fragility of the exposed checkered wood butt is apparent even when fully steel shod like the exquisitely executed Parker on the right. (Coll. Dr. Robert C. Snavely)
Bottom Left, Is the modern narrow-toed butt design correct? This one on a Manton gun (Fig. 39, Bottom) offers a wider surface for recoil absorption. (Abercrombie and Fitch)
Bottom Right, Shooters annoyed by sticky rubber recoil pads who dream of slicker leather-faced ones, may ponder this one coming unglued at heel and toe.

The Butt

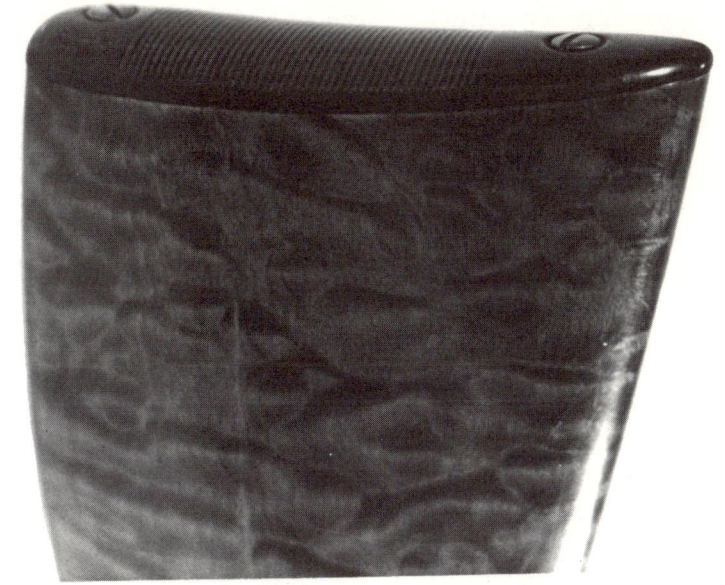

Fig. 2
Left, Sharp edges and a pointed toe make this butt more likely to bruise the shooter's shoulder.
Right, The rounded edges and toe of this buttplate offer no sharp angles hazardous to the shooter during recoil. This design is also probably smoother and quicker in coming to the shoulder.

Many British and European gunstocks are not fitted with buttplates, apparently for aesthetic reasons (Fig. 1, Top). Burrard was so upset by the thought that he declared he would have steel tips installed at heel and toe if the gun were to be subject to the rough usage it would get abroad, a pronouncement which is sufficient justification for the American buttplate.[18] They are available in steel, hard rubber, horn, or plastics and with surfaces that are smooth, grooved, checquered, patterned, or graced by the manufacturer's name or trademark. Hard butt surfaces are happily slick enough not to catch on the shooter's clothing.

Rubber recoil pads are available, varying in consistency from soft to quite hard, and in thickness from about ½ to 1 inch. They decrease the sharpness of recoil impact if they are flexible enough to apply the butt more evenly to the contours of the shoulder notch, especially to the collarbone when shooting high. While they come either roughened or smooth, they all tend to catch on clothing during gun mounting. Their flexibility makes it difficult to get satisfactory results from treating them with gunstock finishing agents as is sometimes recommended for making them slicker. Leather recoil pad covers may come unglued (Fig. 1, Bottom, Right). Pads that are open at the sides collect mud and dirt, but ones closed at the sides may be too rigid. Detachable recoil pads fastened by laces or a stretch sleeve are sometimes used when the shooter wants to temporarily change stock length.

Removable recoil pads, or adjustable buttplates which can be set to shorten or lengthen the stock or change the shoulder-comb relationship vertically and laterally, alter the point of impact of the gun. For reasons discussed in the chapters on the comb and sighting-in, these are as specialized as rifle sights. They offer no substitute for a fitted stock, but may well be used on training shotguns for children. Both buttplates and recoil pads are occasionally separated from the stock by white "spacers," "from which," to quote a nameless savant, "God deliver us." Temporary spacers in the form of washers may be used to test slight changes of pitch or increased length of the stock by placing them under one or both buttplate screws.

4
Pitch

Pitch (English: *stand*) is the relationship between the top-line of the shotgun's barrel(s) or rib and the heel-to-toe line of its butt. In the United States pitch is measured by standing the gun upright with some part of its top-line touching the wall while its butt is flat on the floor. If the barrel(s) are flush against the wall the gun has neutral or zero pitch. If the action touches and the muzzle tilts forward away from the wall it is said to have down-pitch (pitch-down). If the muzzle touches and the action is away from the wall it is said to have up-pitch. Pitch is measured in inches from the wall to the

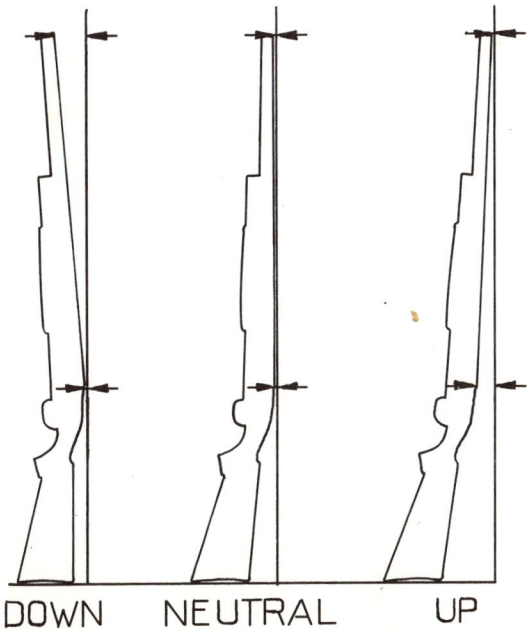

DOWN   NEUTRAL   UP

muzzle or the action. Barrel length and gun type must be specified, if this system of measurement is to be meaningful.

The English describe pitch by specifying measurements from the center of the (front) trigger to the heel and to the toe of the stock.

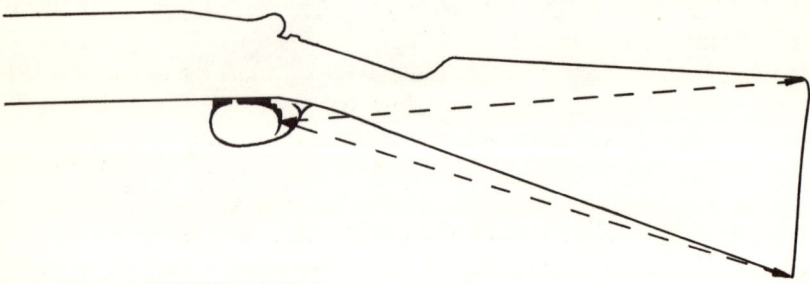

Neither system is entirely accurate for comparing the pitch of different guns. The American system would give about ½ inch more pitch to a 26-inch barreled repeater than to a break-open gun of the same barrel length. Results are inaccurate when the British method compares the pitch of a side-by-side with that of a repeater or over-and-under gun whose trigger is centered about an inch farther below the barrel top-line. A simple method of measuring pitch accurately regardless of other gun dimensions is to measure what pitch is: the angle between a backward projection of the top-line of the barrel(s) and an upward projection of the heel-to-toe line of the butt. This can be done on a tabletop with a folding ruler and a cheap protractor.

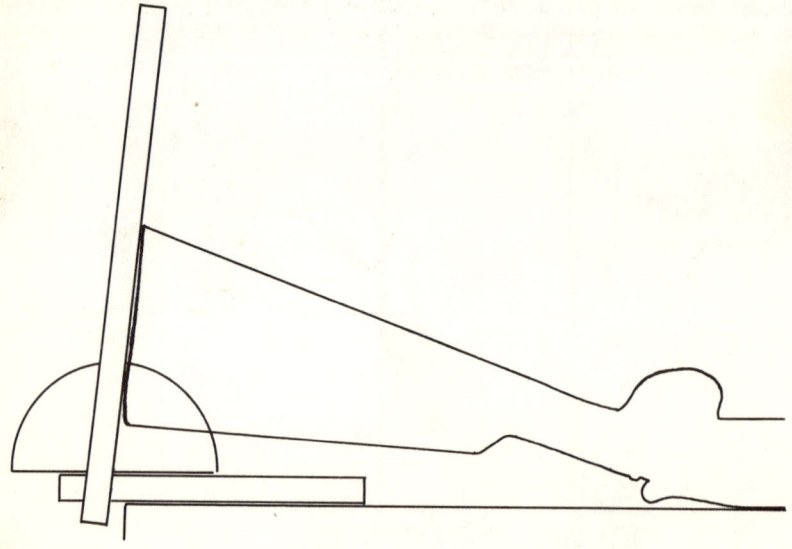

Pitch

The pitch measurements recommended or personally used by some authorities are: Askins,[19] 1¼″-2¼″ down; Churchill,[20] 2″ down; Greener,[21] neutral; Keith,[22] 1″-2″ down; Nichols,[23] 1″-2″ down; O'Connor,[24] 1″-1½″ down (26″ barrels); and Sell,[25] 2″ down. The general range of modern opinion in favor of some down-pitch corresponds to that of factory stocks sold in the United States. Theoretically, pitch should be set at an angle to maintain the maximum surface area contact between the butt and the muscles in the shoulder notch. While some down-pitch does this when the gun is pointed horizontally, the area of contact decreases as the gun is pointed higher. For this reason fit cannot be perfect, and is probably not critical. The angle of down-pitch may be relevant to the amount of discomfort the shooter feels on recoil, since the more down-pitch the sooner the butt will rest against the tender collarbone when shooting at higher angles. Some live pigeon shooters have been successful with neutral or up-pitch, presumably because the projecting toe of such a stock helps them hold high. While this factor may be helpful for some types of horizontal shooting, up-pitched stocks tend to slip off the shoulder the higher the gun is pointed. As discussed in conjunction with recoil, extremes of pitch may have some influence on the gun's point of impact. Payne-Gallwey's discovery that his gun shot consistently low (regardless of wind direction) when fired overhead at a kite target may have been related to pitch.[26]

The correct angle of pitch is best determined by trial and error during actual shooting. The feel of a given angle of pitch may be influenced by the type of curve used to hollow the butt. The exact measurement of pitch angle can enable the shooter to stock different guns to have the same pitch "feel" provided the same type of buttplate or recoil pad is used.

5
Cast

Cast is the generic term used to describe deviations of the buttstock from the midline in either the vertical or the horizontal plane. Seen from above, a cast stock appears to be slightly twisted to one side. Viewed from the rear, the butt slants diagonally because the toe is set farther out of the midline than the heel. This twisting of the stock in two planes is designated cast-at-heel and cast-at-toe and the amount of cast is measured in relation to the center lines of the gun. Cast-off stocks are bent to the right, cast-on stocks to the left. Cast-

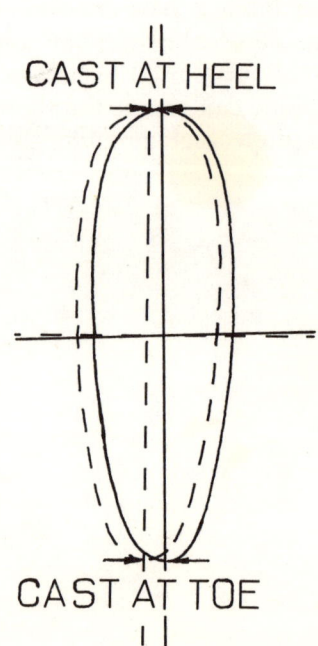

Cast

off is for shooters who mount their guns to the right shoulder, cast-on for those who shoot from the left shoulder. The curvature by which the stock changes direction is usually between its point of attachment to the action and the beginning of the comb.

Commercial guns and gunstocks now manufactured in the United States are generally not provided with cast. European and British authorities and manufacturers always recommend and offer stocks with cast. Hearn[27] and Stanbury and Carlisle[28] consider the average cast-at-heel to be ⅛" and cast-at-toe ¼", Barthold[29] ⅛" and ³⁄₁₆", and Greener[30] ³⁄₁₆" and ⅜". Foreign shotguns made for sale in the United States may be stocked with cast. Americans who purchase a new or used foreign-made gun should be careful to obtain one with a stock cast on or off to suit them. There is, however, no perceptible demand for cast on the part of American shooters. From the American manufacturers' standpoint the introduction of cast would complicate the production and sale of guns by dividing the shooting public into right- and left-handed customers. With the exception of Francis Sell, who indicated his personal preference for ⅜" cast-off, modern American writers have not favored it.[31] Is there anything to it? For reasons that will be developed, cast-at-heel and cast-at-toe seem to be two distinct entities based on different principles. What each has to offer will be examined separately.

The effect of "normal" cast-at-heel, by pivoting the heel of the stock away from the shooter's cheek, is to swing the edge of the conventional side-tapered comb more or less into parallel with the line of sight.

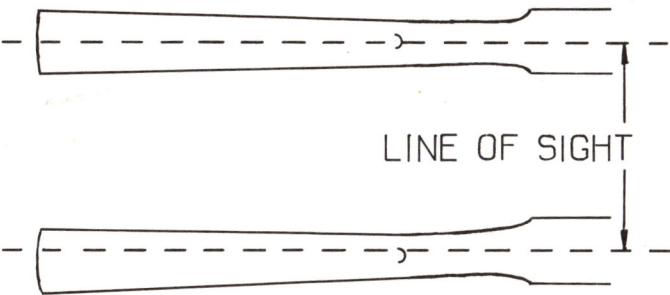

This is rational insofar as it can eliminate error in eye position caused by the movement of the shooter's cheek backward or forward along the side of a tapered stock, as discussed in the chapter on the comb. The shooter's eye, however, may swing too far across the comb. Marked cast-at-heel, or even "normal" cast-at-heel in combination with a very narrow comb, can easily shift the shooter's eye entirely out of the line of sight across the comb. It isn't difficult to imagine that such an exaggeration could bring the opposite eye into play during gun pointing and be one of the causes of the "master eye" problem that preoccupies so many writers on shooting.

As used in practice by British gun fitters, cast-at-heel is set from side to side with the adjustable stock of a try-gun, like the windage dial on a rifle's rear sight, to correct any consistent lateral error in the shooter's gun pointing. This same effect can be more simply achieved without cast-at-heel by eliminating the taper on the side of the stock next to the shooter and carefully fitting the contour of the edge of the comb and the body of the stock to his cheek. An American using a gun with cast-at-heel may be confused by the slight rotation of stance required and by the "out-of-line" feeling of his rear hand on the curved grip. He may even find the comb so far away that he agrees with Keith that it prevents firm cheeking.[32] Shooters who have a problem getting the eye properly placed in line across the comb should consider some degree of cast-at-heel only after everything possible has been done to solve it by modifying the lateral contour of the comb.

Cast-at-toe has a rationale based on a simple anatomical fact. To demonstrate it the shooter should stand in front of a mirror and with his opposite hand press a ruler lengthwise into his shoulder notch as if it were the butt of a gun. Instead of fitting vertically, the ruler will be seen to fit at an angle, slanting in the direction the butt of a gun stocked with cast-at-toe slants away from the midline of the shooter's body. By tilting the ruler upwards the shooter will find that this slant continues to be the natural angle of the butt until the ruler is altogether free of the shoulder notch and rides on the narrow surface of the collarbone, as the butt does when the gun is pointed high overhead. The shooter can confirm this observation with a cast-at-toe-less gun. Push it back slowly into the shoulder notch with firm pressure, but hold it so that it is free to rotate as it goes back. The butt will twist, making the barrels cant out of line.

This canting effect may occur during actual shooting with a stock without cast-at-toe when the gun recoils backward into the shoulder notch before the shot load has left the muzzle. While this backward movement is relatively insignificant with medium caliber rifles (a distance of less than 0.1 inch), it varies between ¼ and more than ⅜ of an inch with shotguns because of their relatively lighter weight and heavier charge. Using Gen. Hatcher's formula, a 6½ lb. shotgun will recoil about $\frac{5}{16}$ inch back into the notch of the shooter's shoulder before a 3¼-1¼ load leaves the muzzle.[33] Cast-at-toe thus seems worthwhile because it enables the butt to fit the anatomy of the

Cast

shoulder and may help to prevent cant during pointing and firing the shotgun.

It is possible to measure the amount of cast-at-toe required by the individual shooter with an improvised pendulum and a helper. First measure the length of the butt to be fitted. Then tape a weighted string to the zero end of a ruler so that the string will hang free below the zero mark down the center of the ruler when it is held upright. Place the ruler firmly in the shoulder notch as before, with the zero mark at the level where the heel of the butt would normally come. The helper can then measure the distance between the pendulum string and the center line of the ruler at the correct distance down the ruler for butt length, which will be the shooter's correct cast-at-toe measurement.

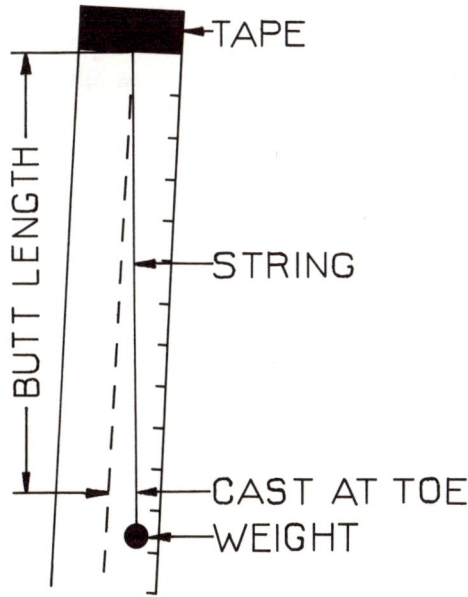

Shooters who may be surprised by the amount of cast-at-toe indicated will be gratified by the ease with which a gun stocked with cast-at-toe comes to the shoulder. If cast-at-toe is used without cast-at-heel, the change in stock direction should begin to the rear of the grip to avoid the twisted feel of the grip of the conventional cast-off stock. Another aspect of cast, its possible effect on the gun's point of impact, is related to recoil and will be discussed later in conjunction with that topic.

6
The Grip

The *grip (hand-grip, small)* is the part of the stock the shooter holds in his near hand. Theoretically, two basic designs are offered: the straight (straight-hand) grip and the pistol-grip. However, when grip design variants are arranged as illustrated, these two types appear as the extremes of a sequence running from the true straight grip to the reverse-curve (Etchen-type) pistol grip.

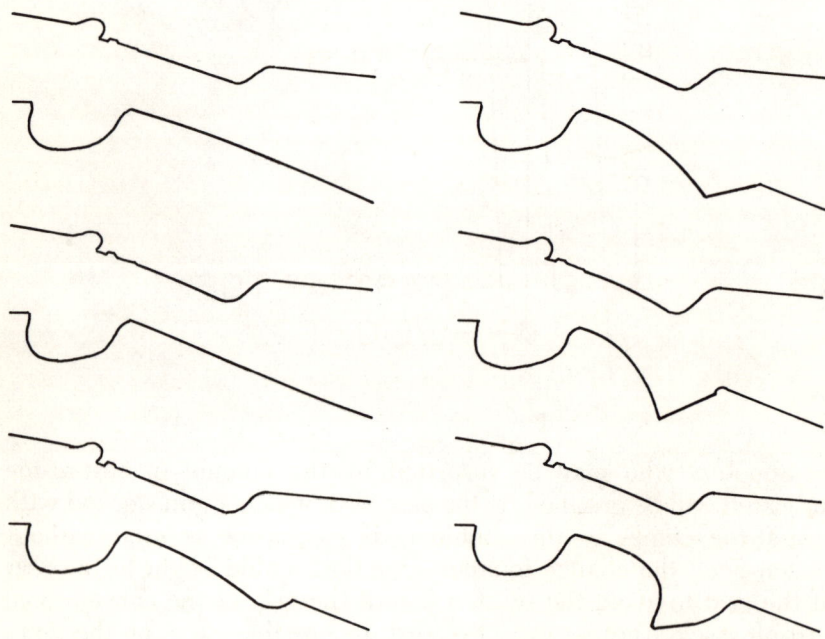

The popularity of many of these styles (straight, half-pistol, full-pistol, and Etchen) over a long period of time indicates that no

The Grip 35

single grip is best to the exclusion of others. The straight grip has been justified as the one most suitable for use with double-triggered guns because the hand could be more easily shifted on it than any other when changing triggers. A surprising number of the authorities who make this statement also disclaim that they personally move their hands when changing triggers. All writers, including this one, tip their hats to the straight grip for making the sleekest looking stock. However, demand for straight grip stocked single-triggered guns by American shooters suggests that they also like their handling qualities. The most comfortable straight grip should have what Col. Peter Hawker describes as ". . . a good fall in the handle, and not be, as some are, nearly horizontal in that part."[34]

Pistol grips become progressively and awkwardly thicker toward the rear as the curve of the grip becomes more pronounced, which may account in part for the greater popularity of less extreme versions. Full and Etchen grips, however, continue to appear on trap guns, perhaps because they are felt to be more helpful in holding the gun level, or in closing the action of a pump gun. The sharp protruding end (cap) of such grips makes them less comfortable to carry in the field. For stockmaking purposes this aspect of the grip can be specified as the angle formed by the (flat) cap of the grip and its underside. The technique of specifying the curve of the pistol grip by measuring the distance from the center of the (front) trigger to the front angle of the grip-cap is only accurate if the length of the underline of the grip is known and its curve is not parabolic or flattened.

The use of pistol grips has some anatomical justification when the gun is held in the fully mounted position. To demonstrate this, grasp a ruler in the grip hand and observe the angle it forms with the arm when the wrist is easy and relaxed. The angle is more or less like that of a pistol grip, about 15 or 20 degrees off the vertical. Now tilt the ruler gradually forward to observe the increasing strain put on the wrist as its angle changes toward that used to grasp a gun with a straight grip. Now, without moving the wrist, move the elbow of the grip hand up and down and observe how elbow position during gun mounting affects the angle of the grip. The higher the elbow is held, the less curvature the grip requires to fit the hand comfortably. The selection of a pistol grip angle that is most comfortable for the individual when his gun is mounted can thus be seen to depend on the elbow position he consistently uses in shooting.

Before choosing any particular grip, the field shooter, unlike the trap shooter, should remember that he is going to spend a great deal more time holding and carrying his gun than pointing it. Prolonged wrist strain from a grip that is uncomfortable to carry all day will ruin his shooting. A little experimenting with a gun will show that the lower the muzzle is pointed during carrying, the more comfortable is a fuller pistol grip; the higher the muzzle is carried, the more comfortable a straighter grip. Some form of pistol grip may be more natural during gun pointing, but whether it will be natural for carrying depends on the angle at which the gun is held. The hunter who carries his gun more or less horizontally across his waist with the end of the pistol grip turned toward him will want it designed not to punch him in the abdomen (Fig. 17). Factors to consider from this standpoint are the curve of the grip, grip length, and the angle formed by the cap and the underside of the grip. Of the latter the obtuse angles possible with less curving grips are most suitable. The end of the grip can be rounded or a rounded grip cap installed.

If the reader has any doubts about the importance of individual grip fit, he is probably not a pistol shooter and might take a look at the catalogs offered by pistol grip makers. The elements of grip fit—length, taper, and cross-sectional shape—must all be adjusted to the individual's hand span and finger length. The length of the grip should be set when the trigger finger is in firing position. If the shooter uses a double-triggered gun, and actually does change his hand position in using both triggers, the length of the grip should be set for the hand position used in pulling the rear trigger. While there is nothing more abominable than a short grip, excess grip length is a nuisance (Fig. 3.). Grip length fit also includes adjustments at the notch of the comb and at the undercut so that thumb position is comfortable during holding and for manipulating a top safety, without permitting the hand to rotate over the top of the grip.

Churchill emphasized the importance of correct grip taper in controlling the gun during recoil.[35] He felt that the grip should be slightly cone-shaped, the thicker end towards the action, a design which would reinforce the shooter's hold when the gun moved backwards on recoil. A modified bulb or submarine shape could serve the same purpose. A grip that tapers in the opposite direction, all too often seen, allows the recoiling gun to slip through the fingers. Even worse than the reverse taper is the occasional wasp-waisted grip, hollowed in the center (Fig. 4.).

Improper grip design or fit, or poor trigger-guard design, may cause the shooter to bruise the middle finger against the back of the trigger-guard. A common fault in commercial grip design is a lack of adequate circumference. The cross section of the grip should be chosen to feel like a comfortable and naturally manageable handful

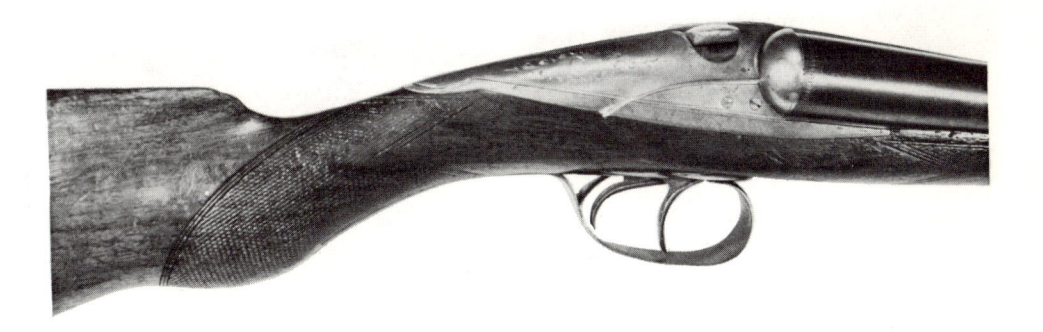

The Grip

Fig. 3
Top, A pistol grip of correct length offers a hold long enough for the entire hand when firing either trigger.
Bottom, A shooter of ordinary hand size must cradle the cap of this awkwardly short pistol grip in the palm of his hand even when firing the front trigger.

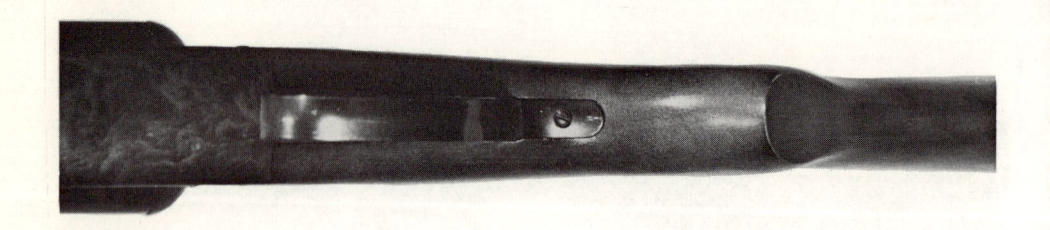

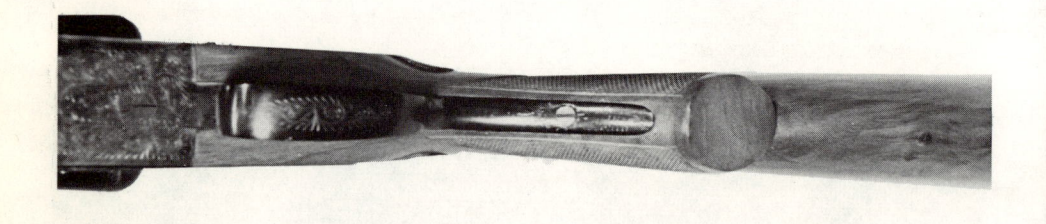

Fig. 4
Top, A correctly tapered grip forms a cone that reinforces the shooter's hold during recoil.
Bottom, Incorrect grip taper will cause the shooter's hold to loosen during recoil.

The Grip

according to the individual's hand size. Gloves should be allowed for if they are generally used with a gun. A grip which forms in cross-section an oval flattened at the sides somehow feels inadequate even when its circumference is actually large. Wider ovals, eggshapes (larger end down), or the rounded diamond cross-section recommended by Burrard feel much better in the hand.[36]

While some of these symmetrical cross-section designs are superior to others, they all ignore the fact that the human hand is not symmetrical. A step in the direction of a grip contoured to fit the individual hand is the "Wundhammer swell," a modest bulge in the vicinity of the base of the index finger, familiar to target rifle shooters (Fig. 22, Left). Free-sculpturing other gently swelling contours can produce an individual hand fit that gives secure gun control no symmetrical grip can offer. Very specialized grips, with thumbholes and precise finger grooves, are not adapted to the hunter's type of gun mounting, whatever their virtues may be for the trap shooter whose gun is at his shoulder before he calls for his target.

The shooter who sets out to redesign the grip of a gun will find his options limited by the rigidity of the upper and lower tangs of pumps and automatics and of the upper tang (strap) of side-by-side and over-and-under guns. Fortunately, the rigid trigger-plate extension of the two latter types is usually short. The trigger-guard tang which covers it and extends to the rear is flexible and can be bent or straightened to adapt to different grip angles.

7
The Fore-end

The *fore-end* (*fore-arm*) is the wood by which the shooter grasps the front of the gun. It is of significance because of the extreme importance of the shooter's extended hand in carrying, mounting and especially in pointing the gun. Yet its design very often has little relation to the gun's handling qualities or to individual fit. Instead of being shaped to help or fit the shooter, as even the standardized factory-made buttstock hopefully is, the factory-end is usually shaped simply to contain its contents and sized to look in proportion with the gun's barrel(s) arrangement and gauge. The mechanical design of the gun's extractor or ejector mechanism, and of the magazine (if it has one) for a certain number and size of cartridges—together with the magazine-operating mechanism—has been allowed to dominate fore-arm design.

The three basic fore-end designs can, for lack of an established terminology, be called the *splinter* that holds the extraction system of side-by-side guns (Fig. 13, Top), the *shell* that wraps around the barrel(s) and the extractor mechanism of over-and-under guns or the magazine system of semi-automatic guns (Fig. 20, Top), and the *handle* that is attached to the magazine and reloading mechanism of pump guns (Fig. 16, Top). Modifications which have been contrived to improve two of these basic designs for the shooter's convenience: the wide, shallow American beavertail fore-arm (Fig. 13, Bottom) for side-by-side guns and the rearward extension of the handle fore-arm of pump guns (Fig. 15, Bottom) are not used so frequently as they deserve. The Colley fore-end for side-by-side guns, simply a deepened but not widened splinter, is rarely seen.

In the matter of the distance between the (front) trigger and the front end of the fore-arm, which permits the shooter to position his hand to balance the gun, gun type has ordained about a 12-14 inch measurement for side-by-side guns, 14-15 inches for over-and-

The Fore-end

under guns, and 16-18 inches for pump and semi-automatic guns; generally regardless of barrel length, gauge, or other factors related to balance. In any case, the splinter fore-end offers no hand-hold and the shooter must grasp the gun by the barrels even at this fore-arm. Many beavertail fore-arms are so short the shooter who wishes to hold the gun further forward is obliged to grasp it by the barrels anyhow. The shooter of the conventional handle fore-arm pump gun, on the other hand, must hold his gun with his arm extended because the handle is set so far forward and there is no place to move his hand backward from the short 6-inch handle.

The hand-hold wrap-around measurements of other than side-by-side 12-gauge guns, composed of differing widths and depths, varies roughly between 5¼ and 6 inches with the design and the manufacturer. However, smaller gauge guns are customarily equipped with fore-arms of smaller wrap-around size, down to as little as 4 inches for many 28 and .410 gauge guns, presumably in the interest of appearance rather than the shooter's hand size. There is no reason why the same shooter should be expected to grasp the barrels over the almost nonexistent fore-end of a side-by-side set close in front of the trigger, the round wiggling fore-end of a pump set far from the trigger, or fit his hand to the fore-end of a smaller gauge gun that is very much narrower and shallower than that of the manufacturer's identical model in a larger gauge.

Since it seems fair to claim that manufacturers offer no fore-end standardized to fit the shooter, an investigation of the human factors affecting fore-arm design and fit seems in order. The shooter generally tries to balance the burden of the gun's weight more or less equally between his hands during carrying. When mounting and pointing, however, the position of the near hand is fixed at the grip while the far hand shifts to control gun balance during shooting. To a considerable extent the "feel" of the gun during pointing depends on the leverage of this extended hand. Its position can make the gun muzzle-heavy, muzzle-light, slower or faster pointing.

Gough Thomas and many accomplished shooters who emphasize the importance of "built-in" gun balance may be assumed to contend that the quality of really good splinter fore-arm equipped side-by-side guns more than compensates for holding them by the barrels.[37] Some of this quality of balance is certainly due to the light weight of the small fore-end, as witness the general lack of enthusiasm on the part of gentlemen of this persuasion for the heavier beavertail fore-end. Balance or possibly aesthetic considerations aside, there seems to be little justification, however, for a fore-end that cannot function as a suitable hand-hold at a position where the shooter can get the best balance.

The first requirement of fore-arm design should be that it extend far enough toward the trigger and toward the muzzle to allow the shooter to shift his hand from the most convenient place for carrying the gun to the place he wants to use when pointing it. A fore-arm designed to oblige the shooter to use the same fore-end hand-hold every time may make gun mounting quicker because the shooter's hand consistently and automatically finds the right place for an optimal gun balance. Two such experimental fore-arms are illustrated (Figs. 20-25). The only successful commercial design that controlled hand placement was the Schnabel (beak) tip used on some L. C. Smith doubles (Fig. 41). This is, in effect, a variant of the stop on the underside of the fore-arm familiar in target rifles, a device that may be modified in various ways for the shotgunner who holds with all four fingers on the off-side of the fore-arm.

Whatever the shooter's choice in regard to hand positioning, the second requirement of fore-arm design is good visibility. The third is good gun control. Visibility demands that the thumb and finger tips be down out of the shooter's field of vision. Gun control demands a fore-arm large enough to fill the saddle of the shooter's hand. These requirements will be discussed together because the same elements of design are involved. The side-by-side gun that must be held by the barrels, obstructs the shooter's view and exposes his hand to cold or hot metal. Although the English leather-covered clip-on fore-arm sleeve solves only the temperature problem, wider adoption of this device in the United States might well make this type of gun more popular for shotgun games and extreme hot or cold weather field shooting (Fig. 5.).

There are two alternative ways to fill the shooter's hand and get his fingers and thumb down out of sight. In general, making the fore-arm deeper is logical for over-and-unders and repeaters, making it wider (the beaver-tail) can serve the same purpose for side-by-side guns. In practice both width and depth have to be increased to some extent for any barrel arrangement to a size that fits the individual's hand. Fit should be concerned with hand size, regardless of gauge or gun type. In either case, it is desirable to keep the tips of the thumbs and fingers down and close to the barrels. Egg or bulb-shaped cross-sections with or without grooves or bevels at the top can accomplish this. The groove is probably better since it can

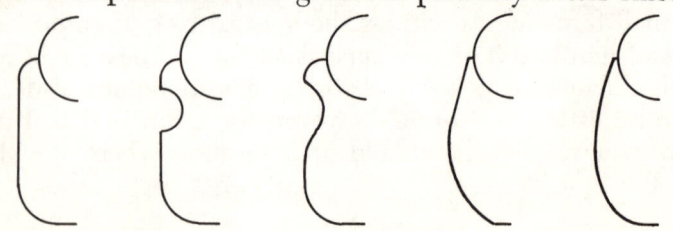

The Fore-end 43

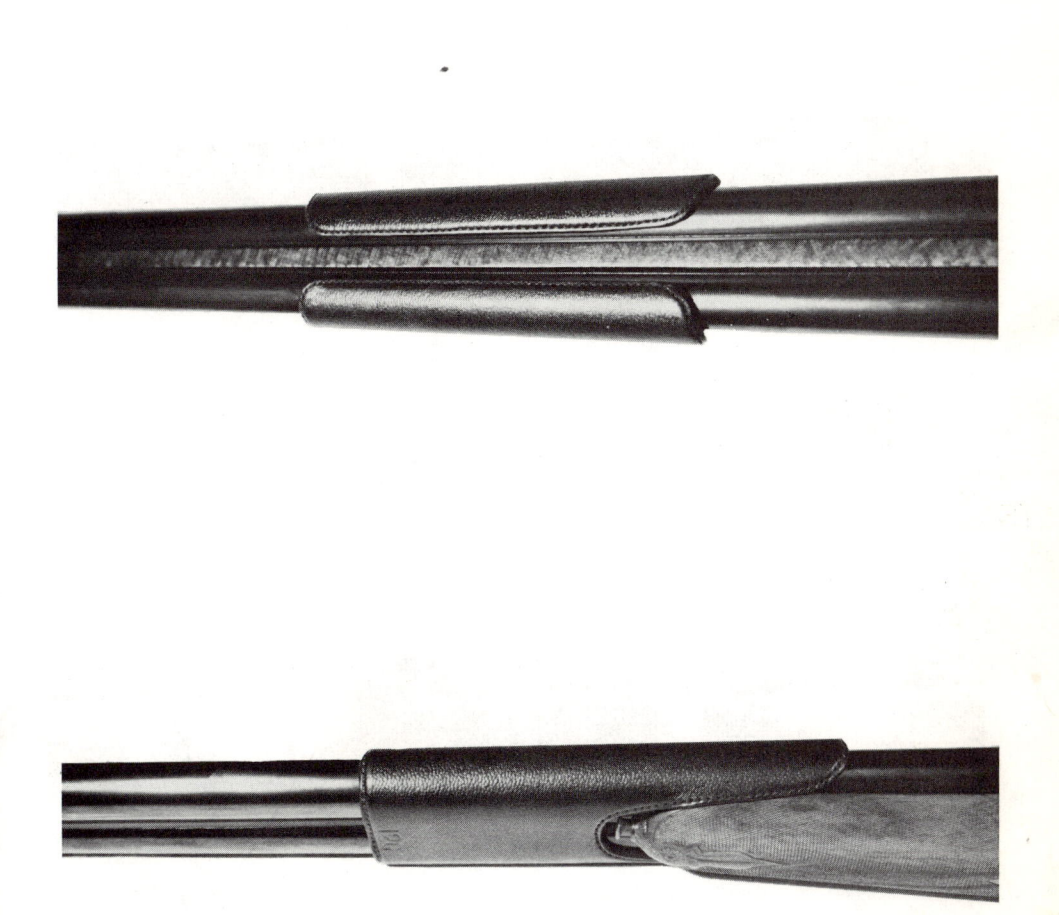

Fig. 5
An English leather-covered spring-clip hand guard can protect the shooter's fingers when the barrels of a side-by-side gun with a splinter fore-end are too hot or too cold. The separation at the top leaves the sighting plane free and the slot at the bottom permits some adjustment to suit the shooter's style of hold. (Abercrombie and Fitch)

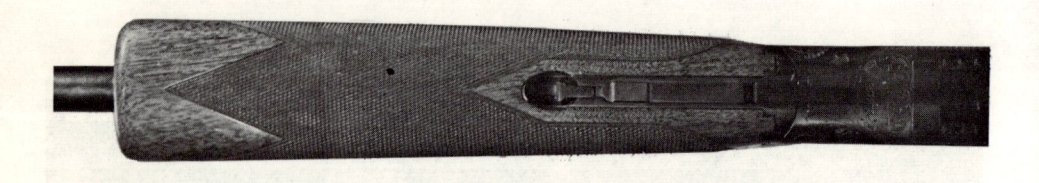

Fig. 6
Top, Correct taper that reinforces the shooter's hold is exemplified in its extreme form by this typical trap fore-end. (Walker's)
Bottom, Incorrect taper that loosens the shooter's hold during recoil characterizes this version of the beavertail fore-arm.

The Fore-end

actively hold the finger tips down and guide them back and forth from carry to pointing hold. While often employed for the deeper shell type fore-arms of over-and-under and repeating guns, the grooves are frequently too small and too sharp-edged.

Recovery from recoil at the fore-arm means the shooter must recover from the upward movement of jump as well as from the gun's backward movement. Good cross-sectional shapes will help him hold the gun down. Recovery from backward recoil will be improved if the fore-arm is tapered so that it is somewhat larger toward the muzzle, as Churchill advocated at the grip. Seen in exaggerated form in some long established trap gun fore-arms, this taper is rather awkward for good looks and bulky for field use (Fig. 6). The principle, however, can be retained and combined with pleasing looks by modifying it into a submarine or streamline shape (Figs. 22, 25).

The shooter who wants to redesign the shell type fore-arm of over-and-under and semi-automatic shotguns has the most adaptable gun types to work with. If the fore-arm of a pump gun is to be extended to the rear, allowance must be made as to how it will relate to the receiver when the pump action is operated. The shooter who wants to have a longer fore-arm on a side-by-side gun should start with a gun whose fore-end is latched centrally instead of by the (Anson) plunger type end latch. If greater depth of fore-arm is also desired the centrally located latch can be recessed, or in some types its internal catch may be lengthened by a gunsmith so that it can be set flush with the wood. Shooters conscious of gun weight can make larger fore-arms lighter by having them hollowed out. In the occasional case where it is desirable to increase forward heaviness lead weights may be added.

8
The Comb

All modern writers agree that the *comb* is the most important part of the shotgun and that fit-at-comb is more important than any other aspect of individual stock fitting. They even agree on the reason why. It is because the comb sets the position of the shooter's eye which *is* the rear sight of the shotgun.

The term comb is used to designate both the angle at the top of the upsweep just behind the grip (point of comb) and the entire top line of the stock (face) from that point to the heel. Drop-at-comb is the vertical distance between a backward projection of the top line of the barrel(s) or rib and the point of comb. It is measured by the same method described for measuring drop-at-heel. The slope of the conventional comb is defined by specifying both drop-at-comb and drop-at-heel, for example: 1½-2½ inches, in that order.

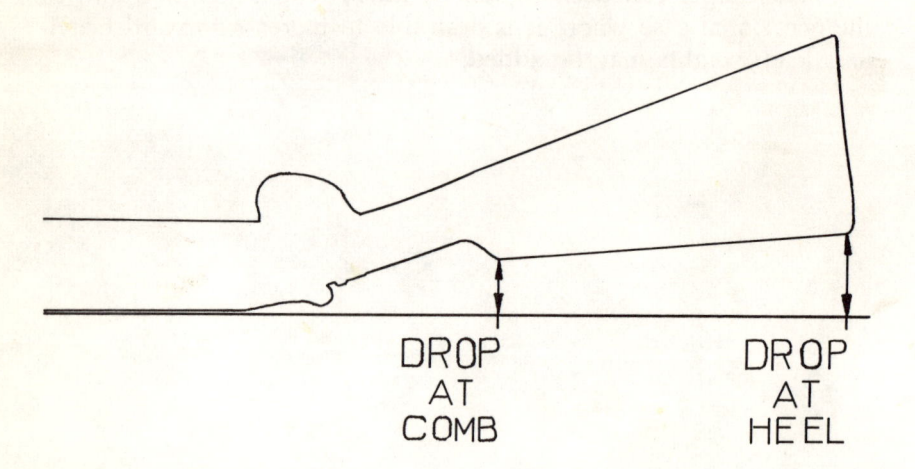

Three measurements are used to describe the comb of the Monte-Carlo type stock: drop at the front and the rear ends of the straight

The Comb

part of the comb and drop-at-heel, for example: 1½-1½-2½ inches.

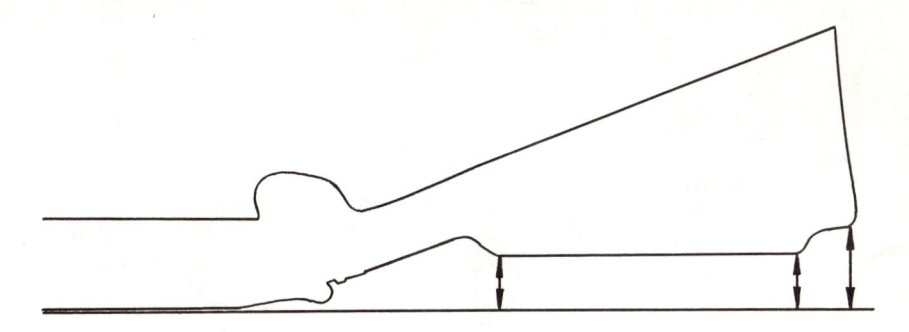

For the record, a review of the measurements of factory stocks of 12-gauge field guns manufactured in or imported into the United States at present writing shows drop-at-comb varying from 1⅜ to 1¾ inches and drop-at-heel from 2¼ to 3¼ inches. However, the vast majority measure 1½" at comb and 2½" at heel (Fig. 7, Bottom). Thus American combs are set higher than in the last century but still average 1 inch in slope (Fig. 7, Top). Barthold describes average German drop-at-comb and drop-at-heel measurements that are almost exactly the same.[38] The average English drop-at-comb is close to ours, but their drop-at-heel is usually less, averaging 2-2¼ inches (Fig. 8, Top). While the system of measurement has been agreed on so that the comb of a given gun can be described, exact comb measurements are meaningful, as will be seen later, only in context with the shooter's own choice of point impact (center of pattern).

Individual fit is concerned with adjusting the gun's comb so that the shooter's eye is in the correct line-of-sight. The line-of-sight is almost never parallel to the top line of the gun. It usually passes above the near end of the action or receiver at a height of about ¼ inch or so, while the height of the front sight is about ⅛ inch, so that projections of the line-of-sight and the top line of the gun

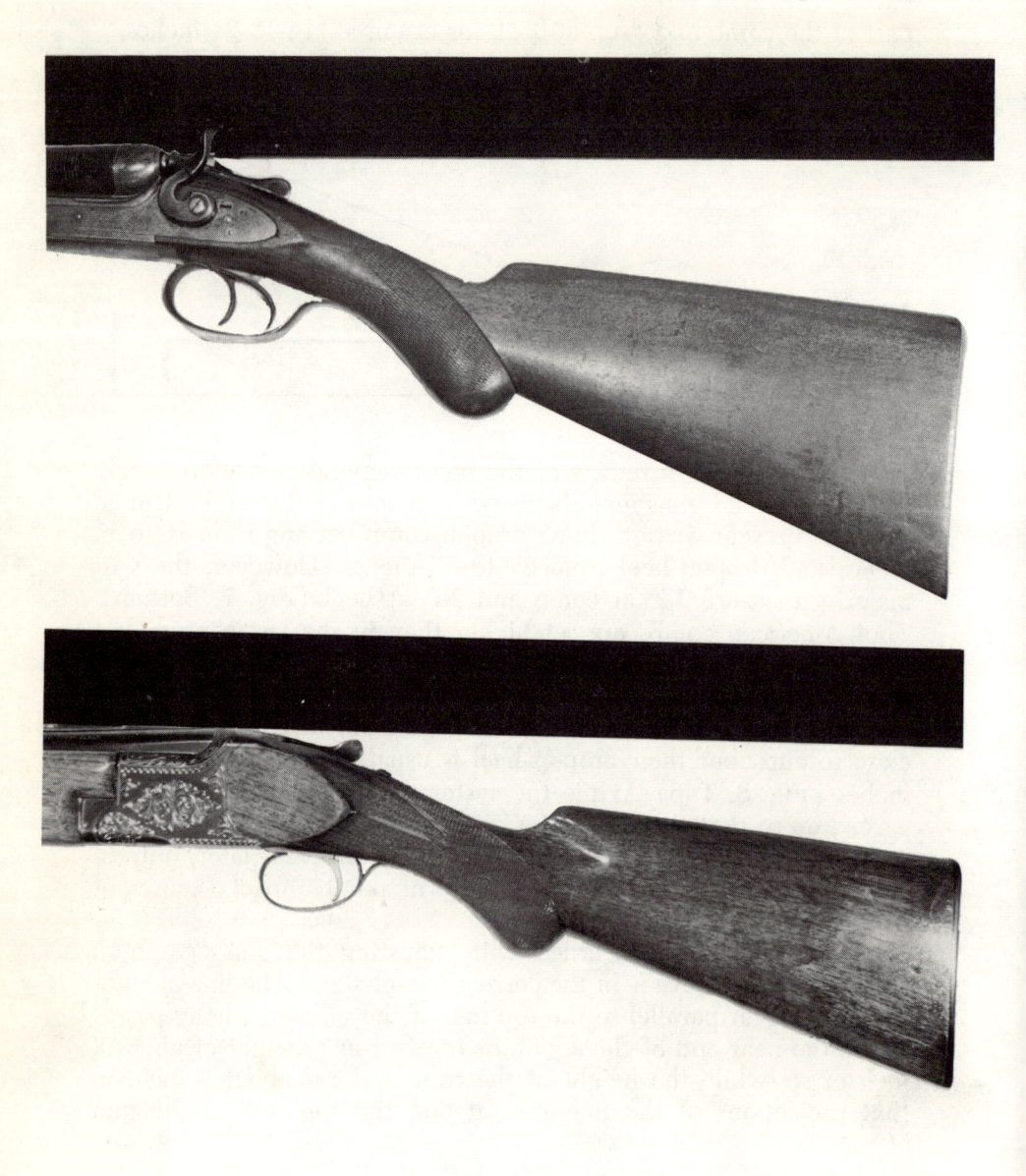

Fig. 7
Top, A very low set, steeply sloping comb on a late nineteenth century American gun by Parker (2″–3″). (Thomas C. H. Webster)
Bottom, A typical modern American buttstock with the most commonly used comb measurement (1½″–2½″) continues the nineteenth-century American vogue for steeply sloping combs, although the contemporary comb is set higher.

The Comb 49

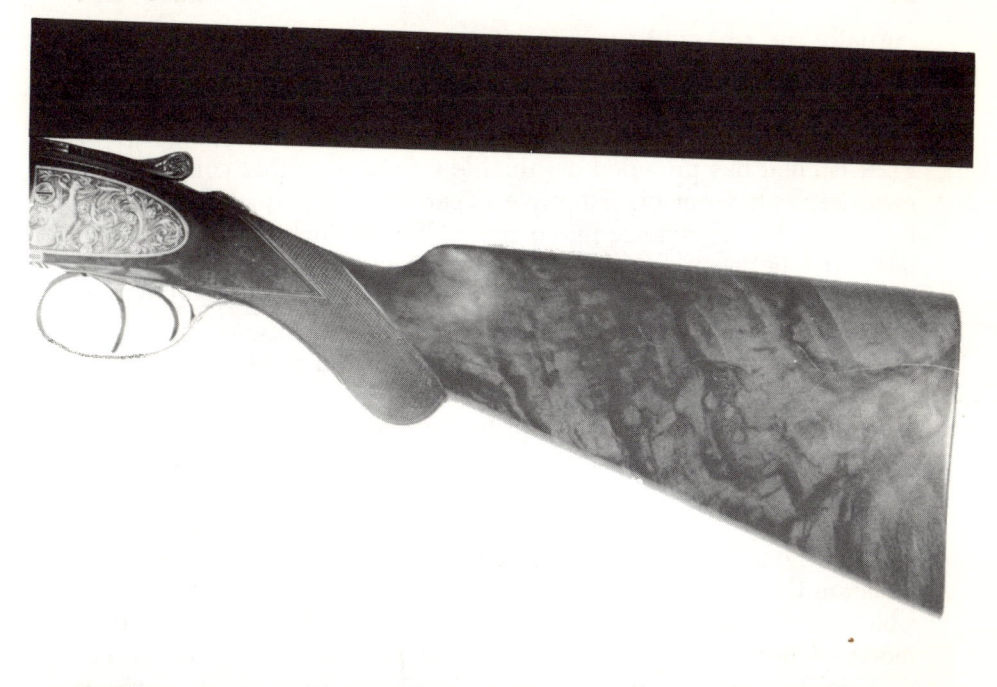

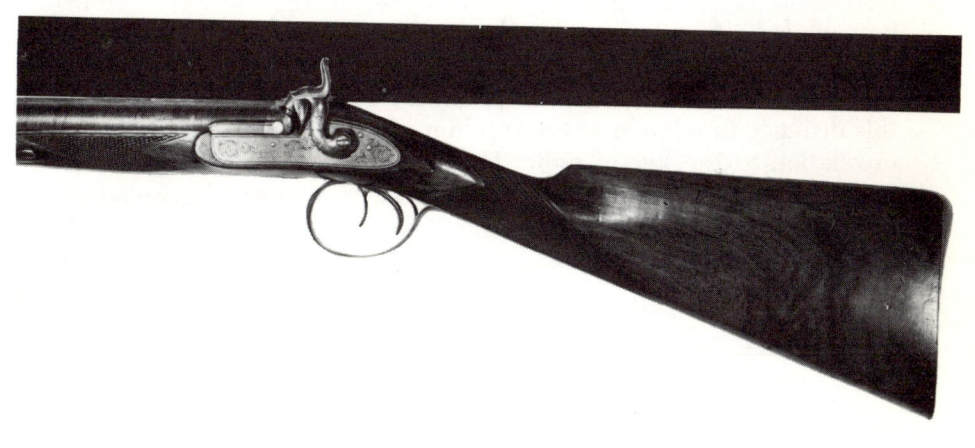

Fig. 8
Top, A modern gun continuing the English practice of a moderate degree of slope at comb (1 ½"–2 ⅛"). (Abercrombie and Fitch)
Bottom, A very moderately sloped comb on an early nineteenth century English gun by Manton (1 7/16"–1 13/16"). (Abercrombie and Fitch)

(usually the rib) will converge at some point in front of the muzzle. The true comb-to-eye distance we are concerned with in fitting is the distance between the shooter's eye in this line-of-sight and the comb.

Fred Etchen has provided a valuable record of actual comb-to-eye measurements from his extensive experience as a stock-fitter.[39] He found no shooter who required more than 1¾ inches. The majority measured between 1½ and 1⅝ inches. From these unique observations actual comb-to-eye distance can be said to vary for different individuals over a range of about ⅜ inch. For a discussion of the significance of this range, the reader is referred to the chapter on the ballistics of shotgun sighting.

The comb-to-eye distance can be compared to the elevation setting for the rear sight of a rifle. If the measurement is right for the shooter, his eye position will be correct for elevation. Sloping combs, however, can be fitted to position the shooter's eye correctly only on condition that the shooter puts his cheek at exactly the same place on the comb every time he mounts his gun. This may be possible for the trap-shooter firing at known targets with his gun mounted before the calls for them, but not for the grouse hunter who has to mount his gun and shoot fast to far right or left, high or low, while he tries to keep his footing among rocks and grapevines. The length of the comb varies between 8 and 10 inches. The typical American sloping comb drops off an average of one inch over this distance in relation to the top line of the gun and slightly more in relation to the line-of-sight. Thus if the shooter's cheek is positioned one inch forward or backward from its correct placement on the comb of the sloped stock, his eye is displaced about ⅛ inch up or down.

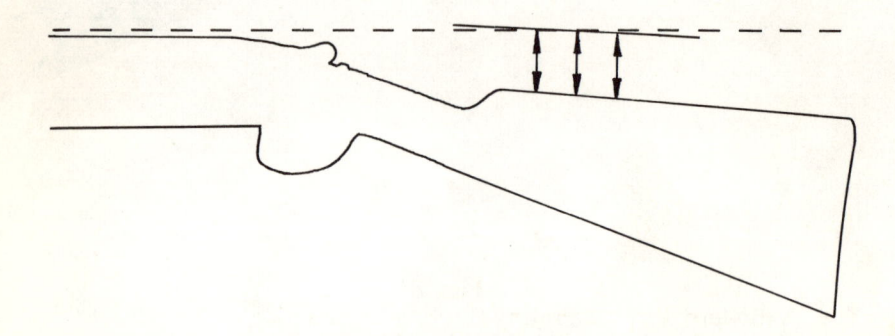

Some displacement also occurs with "level" combs of the type that are only parallel to the top-line of the gun since they slope

The Comb

slightly in relation to the true line-of-sight (Fig. 9, Top). With a comb that is actually parallel to the line-of-sight the shooter's eye will remain in the line-of-sight no matter where his cheek is placed on it (Fig. 9, Bottom). Since there is no specific term for this type of comb, let's christen it the "line-of-sight comb" for the rest of this book.

The obvious gun-pointing advantage of the line-of-sight comb is rarely exploited in the United States, except in some Monte-Carlo buttstocks. The Monte-Carlo has been widely accepted here for trap-shooting but not for field use. Since hunters have as much or more to gain by the use of a line-of-sight comb, it's hard to believe that trap-shooters have overcome any aesthetic objections to the Monte-Carlo while field shooters have not. What probably bugs hunters is the sharp-edged hump at the back of the Monte-Carlo comb—whether it is a real or psychological hazard to fast gun-mounting.

There are at least two neglected designs that can offer the hunter the reliable pointing quality of the line-of-sight comb without the disadvantage of the Monte-Carlo hump. W. W. Greener solved the problem of blending the rear of the comb to the heel of the butt with his "Rational Gunstock."[40] It offers a sufficient length of comb with all the line-of-sight advantages of the Monte-Carlo, but replaces the objectionable Monte-Carlo hump with a safe and pleasing convex curve. The slight convexity of the bottom line of this stock, derived from French and Belgian designs popular before the vogue for the straight-lined English stock, makes the Greener design handsome as well as rational.

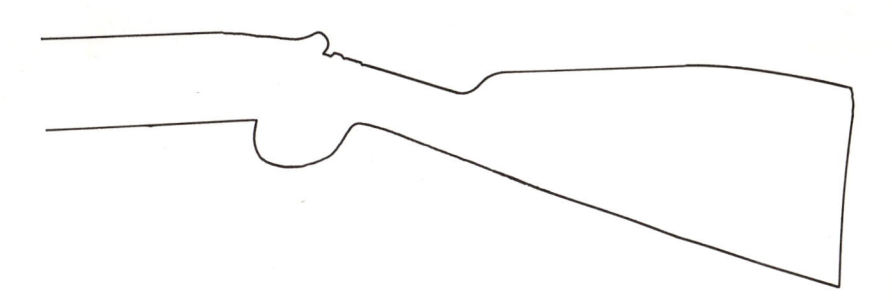

The German hog-back (Schweinsrücken) design offers a slightly longer line-of-sight comb. In this style the rear portion of the comb is straight after it changes angle abruptly behind the level front part of the comb. This straight line together with a straight bottom line from grip to toe gives the hog-back stock a pleasingly rakish look while still bringing the rear of the comb safely down to the heel.

52   The Shotgun Stock

Fig. 9
Top, An American trap gun stocked with a "level" comb (level with the line of the rib), without Monte Carlo, so that the butt is unusually long (5 9/16") and the heel unusually high (1 7/16"-1 7/16"). (Walker's)
Bottom, A true line-of-sight comb slopes slightly upward from front to back in relation to the line of the rib. The gentle curve toward the rear makes a lower heel and a shorter butt possible (1 9/16"-1 5/8"-2¼").

The Comb

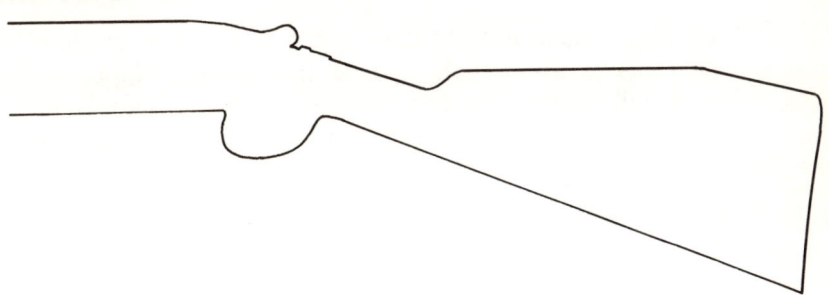

Experimental stocks (Fig. 9, Bottom) can combine the features of these two styles. Another desirable aspect of line-of-sight designs is that because the comb in front of the shooter's cheek is lower than in sloped comb designs, it is less likely to hurt his face when the gun jumps up in recoil.

A compromise solution, more aesthetically pleasing to those who prefer a sloping buttstock with straight lines, is simply to reduce the possible error of the sloping comb by reducing its gradient of slope while still maintaining the correct eye-to-comb distance. This step in the direction of greater shotgun accuracy is long overdue in American stocking practice, though long-established in Britain. On the evidence of the probable dates of manufacture of the ten Manton field guns examined by the author, such dimensions would seem to have been introduced very early in the nineteenth century (Fig. 8, Bottom).[3] On the two earliest guns (dated before 1810) the difference between drop-at-heel and drop-at-comb is $15/16$ and $1 1/16$ inch, while the difference for the later guns (dated 1800-38) varies between $3/16$ and $3/4$ inch. A slope of one-half inch, instead of the present American one inch, would reduce the possible error due to comb slope by 50 percent.

While true comb-to-eye distance sets the elevation of the eye as the rear sight of the shotgun, the side of the comb controls the side-to-side position of the eye. The lateral contour of the comb, with or without a cheekpiece, thus corresponds exactly in function to the windage adjustment dial of a rifle's rear sight. Side-to-side cheek position is affected by two elements of comb design: contour and taper. The contour by which the upper edge of the comb is rounded varies with the gun or stock-maker. Ideally it should correspond to the curve at the underside of the individual shooter's cheekbone, and its thickness be adjusted to place the shooter's eye properly. Most combs taper laterally so that the sides are closer to the center line toward the muzzle. Taper can thus cause the same line-of-sight error with windage that slope can cause with elevation if the shooter's cheek is not in exactly the right position. The gradient of side-to-side taper is about half that of the average slope, so the shooter's eye will be displaced to one side or the other about 1/16 inch for each inch his cheek is out of perfect position forward or backward along the side of the stock.

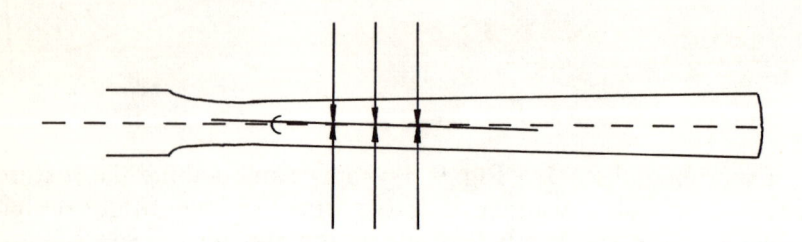

There is thus a considerable advantage to a comb that is not tapered laterally on the side next to the shooter's cheek. A true line-of-sight comb should keep the shooter's eye parallel to the line-of-sight in the horizontal as well as the vertical plane.

The purpose of this chapter has been to introduce the comb by defining its functions and outlining the alternatives of comb design. Individual comb fit will be discussed later in conjunction with sighting-in the shotgun.

9
Cheekpieces

The cheekpiece is not a standard feature of the stocks of American or imported factory shotguns, although German or central European shotguns and shotgun-rifle combinations often come stocked with one. Keith is the only writer who endorses it for field shooting.[41] However, the fact that commercial stockmakers offer a variety of cheekpiece-equipped stocks to fit many shotguns indicates some persistent shooter interest.

The purpose of the cheekpiece is to promote uniform contact between the shooter's cheek and a larger surface area of the side of the body of the stock. The improvement possible can be estimated by comparing the sensation of pressing the hand against the cheek, diagonally edge-on (simulating the ordinary comb), with that of pressing it flat-on and evenly (simulating a well-fitted cheekpiece). It should be remembered that the cheekpiece is not different at the upper edge from any correctly fitted conventional comb. Both the conventional and the cheekpiece-equipped stock fit the cheek firmly just under the cheekbone. The usual stock then gradually slips away from the contour of the cheek below this point, so that contact between the stock and the cheek is soon lost from the comb down. A cheekpiece carefully contoured to fit the individual shooter's cheek offers a wide even-pressured contact with the stock that may increase the accuracy of his gun-mounting, or at least give the feeling of confidence that has endeared it to some trap shooters.

Seen in cross-section, the cheekpiece should extend downward far enough for its lower edge to be below the angle of the jaw. The line of the cheekpiece as seen from above should be straight. The German-descended hollowed-out "saddle" type belongs on target rifles or nowhere, because its high front end may cause facial bruises on recoil. Of cheekpiece designs seen from the side, the oval "pancake" whose upper edge just touches the comb as a tangent is outmoded because it is too short. A better design is the arc-shaped type which merges the upper edge of the cheekpiece with nearly the whole length of the comb. American and Bavarian variations of this basic design can be handsome.

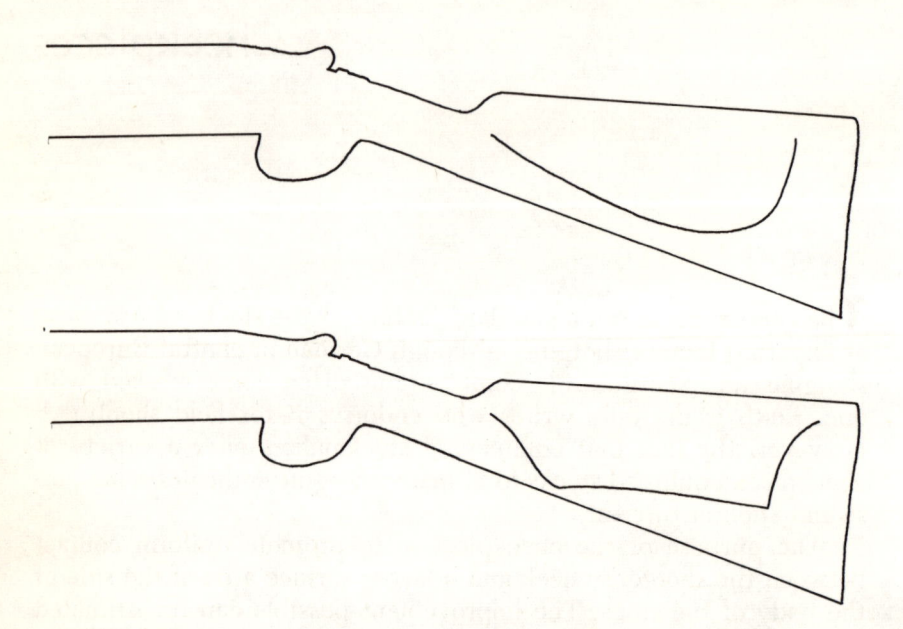

Cheekpieces are often fitted to the Monte-Carlo type of stock. Or a normal stock can be remodeled into a Monte-Carlo by adding a cheekpiece so that its upper edge is elevated above that of the existing comb (Fig. 10). Semi-finished cheekpieces are available. Conventional cheekpiece designs have the disadvantage of a sharp, protuberant rear edge. This hazard to the shooter's face has discouraged their use in the field. They can be made suitable for fast gun-mounting by gradually tapering the rear edge toward the side of the stock in a gentle curve or bevel, eliminating the usual undercut and sharp edge.

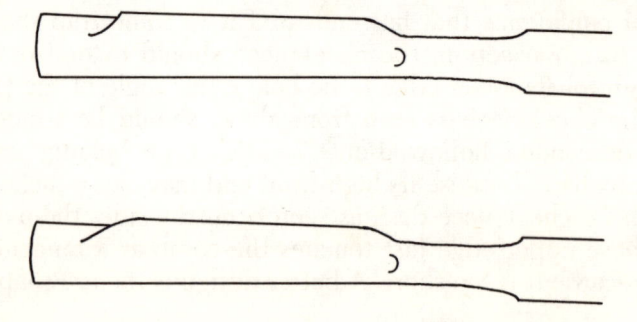

Cheekpieces

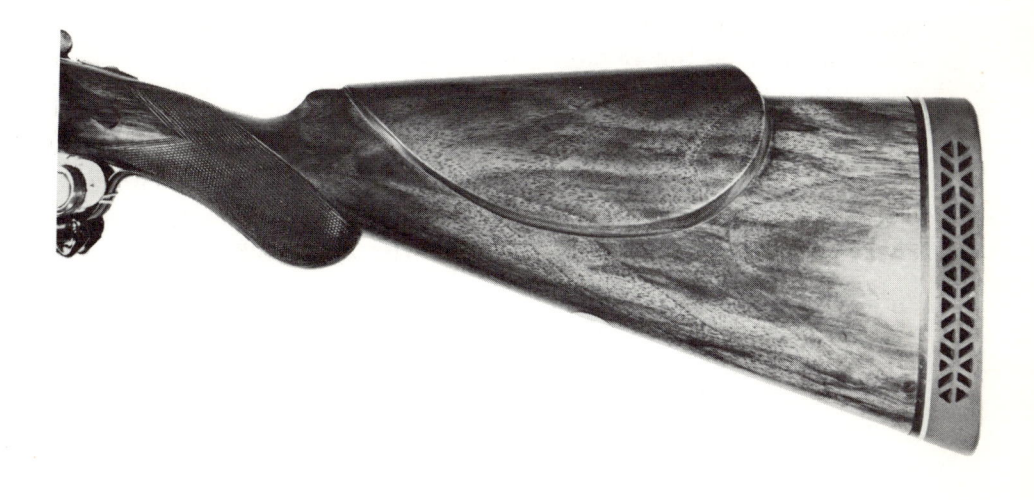

Fig. 10
The added cheek-piece which converts this stock into a Monte-Carlo is an example of very successful stock remodelling. The applied wood is well fitted and its figure is well matched to the wood of the original buttstock. (Abercrombie and Fitch)

A design of this type is pictured in Fig. 25.

The term *roll-over cheekpiece* refers to a modification of the side of the comb opposite the cheekpiece occasionally seen on the Monte-Carlo stock. Instead of the usual rounding, the off-side is undercut to form a sharp lip just below the comb. The roll-over seems to offer no functional or aesthetic advantage, and the sharp edge is a nuisance when the gun is carried (Fig. 17). Removable lace-on cheekpieces are of questionable value because they are not shaped to fit the individual.

Once a good cheekpiece design is selected the fitting of its lateral contour must be done by trial and error. The cheekpiece should always be fitted in conjunction with or after fitting the comb.

10
The Body of the Stock

The triangular body of the stock, below the comb and between the grip and the butt, deserves more attention than it gets. Perhaps it is neglected because it is only thought of in relation to its main business: the support of the functioning parts of the stock around it. However, the body of the stock plays several other roles. It affects the balance of the gun because it contains more weight of wood than any other part of the stock. It controls the thumb position of the grip hand through the design of the undercut. And (in the absence of a cheekpiece) the shape of the cheek side of the stock is important in positioning the shooter's eye.

More than half the total wood on the gun is in the body of the stock. When it is desired to reduce or redistribute the weight of the gun for the sake of convenience or balance, the body of the stock is the easiest and safest place to remove wood. This is generally done by hollowing out the inside. Weight can also be reduced from the outside my modifying the design of the flat sides. A good deal of wood can be removed without any sacrifice of strength by making the sides slightly concave lengthwise (as seen from above), and by making them taper more sharply toward the bottom line of the stock.

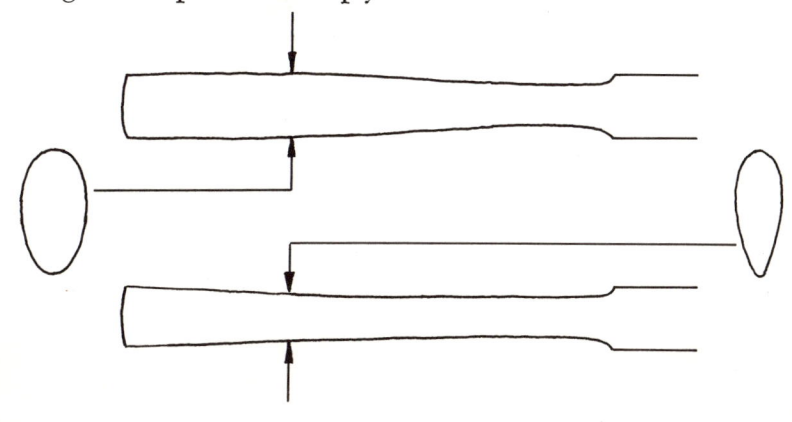

These features can be combined with hollowing out the interior of the stock, or may be used alone where there is any question about the strength of the wood after hollowing. Stocks that are slightly concave lengthwise may help broad-chested, heavy-armed or bulkily clothed shooters in fast gun-mounting.

The eighteenth-century "roach-bellied" design both adds and subtracts wood from the body of the stock. Its sides are slightly channeled out along a diagonal line from the rear of the grip to the butt. That part of the stock below this indentation is made bulbous instead of the usual taper, so that the buttstock in cross-section looks like a somewhat bottom-heavy hourglass. Its appearance is pleasing but execution is difficult, increasing the cost of the stock.

The undercut on the off side of the body of the stock, just below and behind the point of the comb, is important in individual gun fitting. The deeper the cut, the more the shooter's hand will tend to twist around over the top of the grip. The correct degree of concavity acts as a stop to the base of the thumb to keep the hand from rotating out of correct position. Fit at the undercut thus sets the angle of approach of the shooter's near hand to the stock. The position of the notch at the beginning of the comb should be adjusted backward or forward at the same time as the undercut is fitted. Both trigger and safety position should be taken into consideration. Having any undercut on the side nearest the shooter serves no purpose except to make commercial stocks symmetrical for appearance' sake, as well as salable to both right- and left-handed shooters.

The cheek side of the body of the stock should be carefully shaped to fit the individual's facial contour. Its fit is only slightly less important than the height and curve of the comb itself. The shooter should know by the feel of it that his face is held against the side of the stock the same way each time he mounts his gun.

III
SHOTGUN CONTROL AND ACCURACY

11
Balance and Recoil

Though by no means the only player on stage, the stock has a considerable role in both gun balance and recoil. Each of these aspects of the gun will be considered separately with enough background material to make sense of the principles involved.

More technical discussions of balance are to be found in Burrard[42] and Gough Thomas.[43, 44] Gun balance is often spoken of in terms of the *point of balance*. A gun can be placed on a pivot or suspended by a cord, and some point of balance determined a few inches ahead of the trigger. The point acts as an invisible axis upon which the gun rotates when handled by the shooter. A balance point closer to the trigger is generally associated with the desirable field handling qualities of two-barreled guns. Guns having more or less the same balance point, however, do not necessarily have the same "feel." The gun may be imagined as a kind of seesaw on which various weights are placed at various distances on either side of a balance point. It can then easily be appreciated that an infinite number of combinations of weight-distance factors could be used to maintain equilibrium, any given weight taking effect in relation to its distance from the balance point. Simplified diagrams illustrating possible extremes of weight distribution make it easy to understand that the closer to the pivotal point the concentration of the same total weight involved in the balance, the more easily the inertia of rotation, or gun handling, can be overcome.

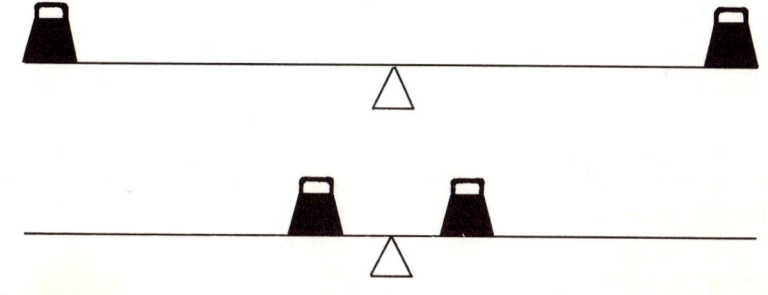

This general principle applied to the shotgun explains the faster swing possible with guns that concentrate their weight near the balance point—such as the over-and-under or the side-by-side—and the slower steadier swing of most repeaters whose receivers and magazines spread their weight farther from the point of balance. Increased overall gun length (with the same barrel length) due to the long receiver of repeaters also results in a marked difference in balance between these two groups of guns.

It should be emphasized, however, that there is no such thing as ideal gun balance. There is only a gun that balances perfectly according to the shooter's individual taste and purposes. Few shooters pay enough attention to choosing a gun for its balance, often sacrificing balance to a preference for a certain barrel length or a certain type of action. Once having purchased a particular gun the buyer is stuck with whatever qualities of balance it possesses as far as the metal gun is concerned. The compensatory method of controlling balance by shifting the position of the hand on the fore-arm has its limits. A hold too close to the trigger reduces gun control and makes the gun muzzle-heavy. A hold too close to the muzzle, as Nichols[45] and Lancaster[46] point out, tends to check swing. The factory fore-arm of a given gun may or may not be suitably designed for the shooter's hand at the place he decides he should hold it to balance and handle it best. A longer fore-arm may offer a better hold, or special shaping may help mark the grip area to promote consistent hand positioning.

Another method of changing the gun's balance by stock modification is to add, subtract, or shift stock weight. The available alternatives are: shortening or lengthening the buttstock, changing to a stock of a lighter or heavier wood, and hollowing or weighting the fore-arm or buttstock. Considerable effects can be achieved without significant total weight change, for balance can be altered appreciably by merely changing the location of weight. Hollowing the butt, a common feature of the stocks of British and European guns, or narrowing its sides can usually be done without loss of structural strength. There is no reason why a long heavy beaver tail fore-end cannot be hollowed and some improvement in balance achieved. Small lead weights can be used alone in the fore-arm or the buttstock, or in combination with hollowing, to change the distribution of weight. A lighter stock wood can be chosen simply to reduce the total weight of the stock or to redistribute weight in conjunction with hollowing or weighting. "French" and Claro are often somewhat lighter than other walnuts. Sycamore, Oregon maple, and lacewood are 10 to 15 percent lighter. Unexpectedly light blanks of a normally heavy wood can sometimes be found. A larger selec-

Balance and Recoil

tion of heavy wood is available if it is desired to increase stock weight.

Recoil is most obviously related to the gunstock because the stock transmits its force to the shooter. The stock can help to reduce recoil effect in several ways. Butt, grip, and fore-arm design factors have already been discussed. Adding to stock weight by methods suggested above will reduce recoil. Readers interested in specific figures on the relationship between gun-weight, ammunition, and recoil should look up Boughan's simple and excellent "Shotgun Recoil Nomograph."[47] Whatever the merits of their design, recoil-absorbing devices to be inserted into the buttstock seem to achieve some of their recoil reduction by adding about half a pound to stock weight. One American manufacturer offers a two piece spring-operated anti-recoil stock similar in principle to that of the Rigby One-Arm stock described under special stocks, but with the advantage that the springs are housed inside the two overlapping pieces of the plastic stock. Independent tests indicate that this system is at least more effective in recoil reducing than is a gun with a gas- or recoil-operated action without this device.[48] The telescoping plastic stock, however, has the disadvantage of not lending itself to changes that may be necessary for proper stock fit.

Recoil has a less apparent effect on shotgun sighting and fit-at-comb due to the behavior of the barrel(s) of a shotgun before the shot charge has left the muzzle. Both shotgun and rifle shooters should be thoroughly familiar with this neglected aspect of recoil, which is dealt with here in relation to the shotgun stock. It is extensively treated by Burrard[49] and Whelen.[50] While the major force of recoil is exerted backward against the shooter's shoulder, some of this force is diverted in ways that concern us here. It may be divided into three components: jump, flip, and vibration.

Jump, familiar to all shooters, is the upward thrust of the muzzle as the fired gun rotates upward on the axis of the shooter's shoulder at the same time as it recoils backward. The angle of the stock in relation to the barrel(s) is the cause of this movement's direction. If the butt were exactly in line with the barrel(s) it would oppose the force of recoil in that line only and no jump would occur.

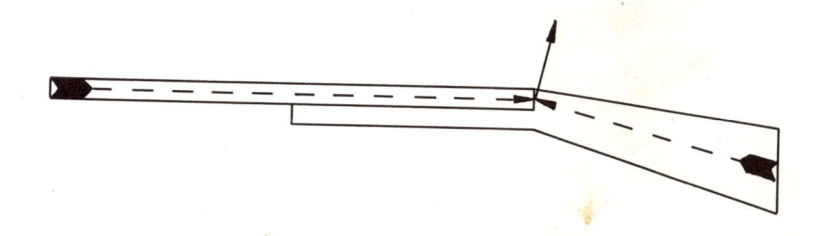

Since the butt is below this line, it opposes recoil with a resistance operating at an angle to the force of recoil. The sum of these two vectors directs some force upward, causing jump.

The angle of this force of resistance is thus seen to be governed by the stock measurement drop-at-heel. Greater drop-at-heel will increase the angle between barrel(s) and stock and increase the upward force of jump. The upper barrel of an over-and-under shotgun would thus shoot to a higher point of impact (pattern center) than its lower barrel for the same reason.

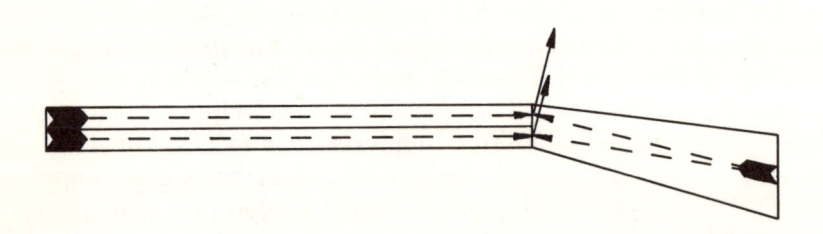

In some cases more or less pitch may alter the gun's point of impact by, in effect, changing the part of the butt that receives the force of recoil. Gough Thomas has pointed out that the physical principles underlying jump also apply to guns that are stocked with cast.[51] The angle between the forces of recoil and resistance is, of course, much less and operates in the lateral rather than in the vertical plane. A cast-off stock would thus cause single-barrel or over-and-under guns to shoot slightly to the left.

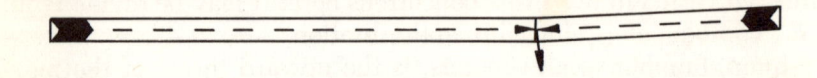

A side-by-side gun's left barrel would shoot to the left but its right barrel will not since it is actually more or less in line with the cast-off butt.

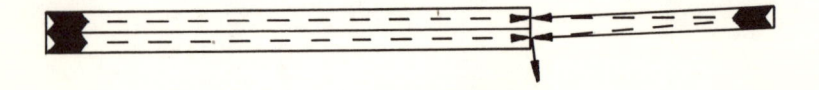

It should be emphasized that those factors which may cause the barrels of two-barreled guns to "shoot apart" can and should be compensated for in the process of barrel regulation during manufacture.

Balance and Recoil 67

Unfamiliar, because unseen, are the downward "flip" or bending of the barrel(s), and the vibration of the barrel(s), which occur at the same time as jump. Both flip and vibration are due to the slight but significant flexibility of the steel of the barrel(s). The downward flip is due to the relative inertia of the muzzle end of the flexible barrel(s) during the upward movement of jump—an action like that of the tip of a fishing rod when it is raised abruptly. The wave movements of barrel vibration are governed by all the metallurgical, mechanical, and ballistic factors involved in the gun and its firing.

All three of these movements affect the direction of the shot charge as it leaves the muzzle. Jump directs the shot charge up, the downward flip of the barrel(s) directs it down, while the timing of the vibration of the barrel(s) may direct the shot charge otherwise. The final line of flight of the shot charge, the resultant of these three vectors, is different from the bore-sight line.

The flip effect is more pronounced in side-by-side guns because of their greater flexibility in the vertical plane. Burrard cites results for this phenomenon, for example, as a point of impact 9-12 inches below the bore-sight line in shooting tests with one 30-inch barreled side-by-side gun at 40 yards. However, as the barrel length of such a gun is shortened, barrel rigidity increases and flip effect diminishes with the result that it "shoots higher." With over-and-under guns the flip component of barrel flexibility is suppressed by rigidity in the vertical plane so the jump component becomes dominant, with the result that the shot charge tends to be thrown upward as it leaves the muzzle. With single-barreled guns the final direction of the shot charge is influenced by individual gun and barrel design. While some general principles do apply to this problem, it should be understood that the vector sum of jump, flip, and vibration is an individual characteristic of each gun and that each gun's true point of impact can only be determined by trial. This also applies to a change in barrel length or gauge; or internal sleeves, new, or extra barrels with the same gun.

Of equally great practical importance to the sighting-in of a particular shotgun is that a change in point of impact may occur when firing loads of different strength. As described in general terms by Gough Thomas for side-by-side guns, the gamut from very light to very heavy loads may successively depress the point of impact up to as much as ten inches at 40 yards.[52] Increasing the powder and shot will simply increase the forces involved in barrel behavior previously described. Analogous lateral deviations caused by cast also vary with different strength loads. While this generic rule is true for side-by-side guns, wide variations may again be expected to occur for individual guns, and all bets are off regarding changes in the point of impact of other types of guns through the same range of cartridges. The author has been unable to reproduce the depression of point of impact reported for side-by-side guns with a number of over-and-under guns, suggesting that the flip phenomenon is predominantly the cause of this change of point of impact in side-by-side guns. Each shooter must determine his own gun's point of impact with the cartridges he intends to use. In order to do intelligent stock fitting, in the sense of shotgun sighting, he must be as wary of the effect of changes in ammunition as any rifleman.

In a practical way, the significance of barrel behavior during recoil is that every shotgun is a different sighting-in problem. Its point of impact must be determined by trial, and the comb of its stock fitted so that the shooter's eye is in the correct position to give the desired point of impact for that particular gun, with a particular load.

12
Special Shotgun Stocks

The purpose of this section is to review the possibilities of special shotgun stocks in relation to the circumstances that may justify their use. Special stocks can be divided into two general classes: those designed to help physically handicapped shooters, and those designed for use by normal shooters for a special purpose.

For the man addicted to the pleasures of the shotgun, their premature end because of physical or optical handicap is a little death. If he is to continue to shoot in spite of them, he must somehow be able to do so safely and hit often enough to continue to find the sport worthwhile. Tremendous advances in plastic- and neurosurgery, orthopedics, and physiotherapy during the last decades may benefit the handicapped shooter who obtains the advice of the best medical specialists concerned with his particular problem. However, with whatever medicine can do for him, or with whatever special stocks or other devices he may use, the shooter is the one who is going to have to learn to shoot all over again on new physical or optical terms. Examples of dramatic achievements by many individuals who have had the patience and will to rehabilitate themselves in physical skills after disabling injury or disease have been widely publicized, but it is hard to convey the intensity of their efforts or the frustrations they have overcome.

If it is possible, the handicapped shooter should consider the advantages of retraining or adaptation without the use of any special contrivance. A classic case in point is that of the normally right-handed shooter who has lost the use of his right eye. Perhaps the most difficult solution is for the shooter to learn to shoot from his left shoulder. The process may be every bit as awkward as it is for a right-handed person to learn to write clearly and fluently with his left hand. But in the long run this may well be the simplest solution and make for the best shooting. Many normal shooters, including Francis Sell[53] and the famous trap-shot Joe Hiestand,[54] have taught themselves to shoot ambidextrously just for the hell of it. The champion is probably Sir Victor Brooke who in 1885 shot 740 rabbits in one day. He fired 1000 cartridges, mounting his gun on his right shoulder half of the day and to his left the other half.[55]

The loss of the sight of the dominant eye is common enough that several special stocks and offset sighting devices have been developed to help the shooter who is daunted by the idea of learning to shoot from the wrong shoulder. Such stocks or sights are designed to bring the opposite eye into the correct line of sight, while the gun is still mounted to the familiar shoulder. Older English stock designs consist either of an exaggeration of cast-at-heel, or an S-curve ("gooseneck," "dog-leg") at the grip, sufficient to move the comb far enough over, either obliquely or straight (Fig. 11). The American "cross-over" stock, credited by Nichols to Lou Smith of the Ithaca Co., is commercially available.[56] It offers the advantage that the buttstock and grip are in the normal line in relation to the barrels. Its saddle-shaped comb permits the shooter to lean his cheek across it to bring his opposite eye into correct sighting position (Fig. 12). However the fact that the shooter's cheek rests diagonally across the top of the comb brings more recoil to bear on his face than do the English types.

Offset sights were invented by Greener and an offset rib by Frank Hogan and fabricated by Howe.

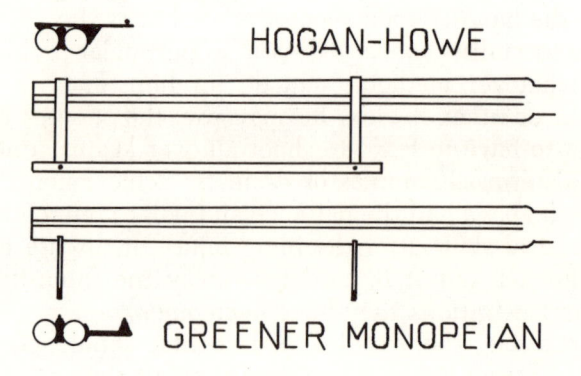

HOGAN-HOWE

GREENER MONOPEIAN

The quality of shooting that can be achieved with the offset principle is suggested by Mr. Hogan's run of 147 at trap.[57] It is probably significant that this particular record was made at trap shooting, for offset sights seem unhandy for carrying or mounting the gun in the field.

The help that stock modification can offer the physically handicapped shooter has to be evaluated in relation to how far training alone can be expected to go. Individual problems are different and

Special Shotgun Stocks 71

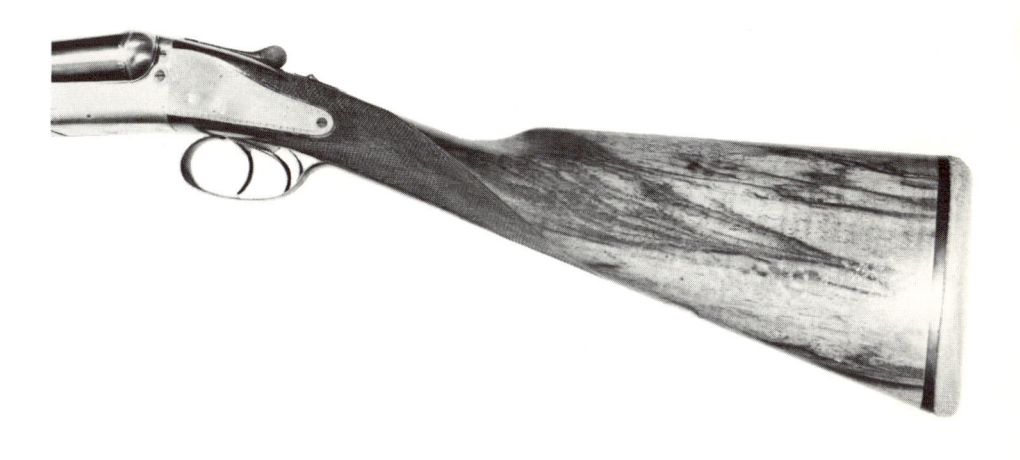

Fig. 11
This cross-eyed stock appears normal from the side but from above describes an S-curve which brings the shooter's left eye into the line of sight when the gun is mounted to his right shoulder. The shooter's head position is the same as with a normal stock. (Abercrombie and Fitch)

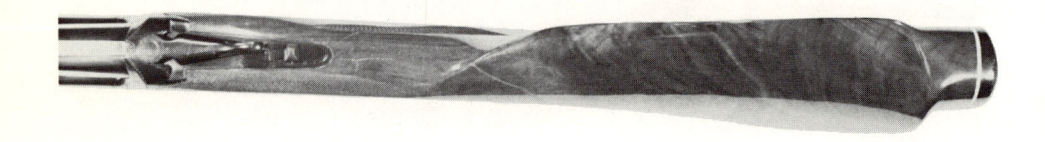

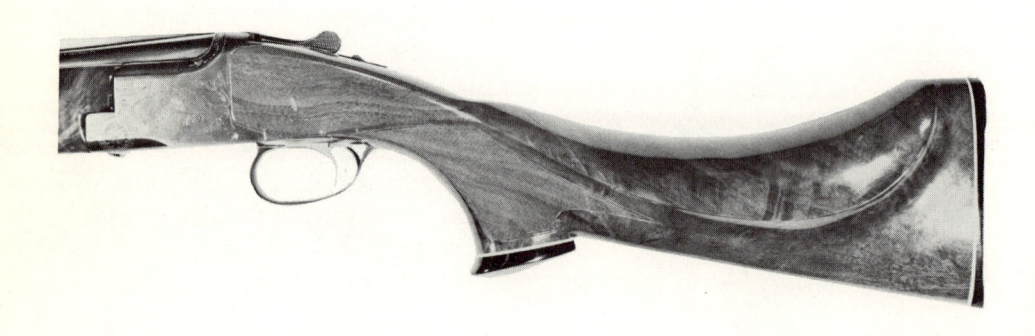

Fig. 12
The butt of this Lou Smith crossover stock is in the normal position so that the shooter must lean his head across its wide saddle to bring his left eye into the line of sight. (Abercrombie and Fitch)

Special Shotgun Stocks

so are their solutions. Consider the problems of amputation or loss of the use, of fingers, a hand, or an arm. No standard designs are available as in the case of the loss of an eye. The shooter must try to analyze his situation and decide whether he needs a special stock (and perhaps design such a stock himself) or can beat his handicap on retraining alone. In some cases a special stock may only be a part of a specially designed gun. The shooter who wants to rebuild a gun should enlist the best gunsmithing help he can get. The prototype gun and stock design (not commercially available) for the amputee is the Rigby "One-Arm" gun. It was a side-by-side, equipped with a sub-machine gun type grip and trigger under the fore-arm in place of the normal trigger and grip, and an open spring-recoil buttstock designed to be pointed and fired with one hand only. George Moeller in 1968 used an American semi-automatic rebuilt on these lines to break 4550 16 yard targets, averaging .9501![58]

With the possible exception of those remarkable gentlemen who make fantastic trap scores from a wheel chair or a crutch, handicapped shooters are not necessarily restricted to the traps. What can be accomplished by a normal game shooter using only one hand without a special gun is indicated by Teasdale-Buckell's description of the performance of the King of Portugal at Sandringham.[59] He shot 200 Pheasants in 35 minutes, mounting one gun to his left shoulder, changing guns, and mounting the next to his right shoulder. Either gun was pointed with one hand only, leaving the other free to speed up the changing of guns! What can be accomplished by a handicapped game shooter using one arm with a normally stocked but specially balanced weapon is best exemplified by Lord Gough, who was rated as one of the best British shots of his day. No allowance was made for his handicap, as witness the title of an article about him, "Are Two Arms Necessary for Shooting?"[60] If the idea of recoil-effect without a hand on the fore-arm seems alarming, it should be remembered that shooting with one hand without shouldering the gun at all has been recommended by more than one authority to give the beginning shooter a feeling of confidence about recoil.

The individual handicapped shooter must analyze his situation and improvise. If one shooter has lost all or part of his trigger finger, should he learn to pull the trigger with his middle finger? Does he need to modify the gun's grip if he does so? Or should he learn to shoot from the other shoulder? If another shooter resolves to learn to shoot with one hand, what barrel length, balance, gun weight, and gauge will be best? Should he use a Rigby One-Arm type gun or a thumb-hole stock with a sharply recurved pistol grip? If a shooter's fore-arm hand has been mangled, will he devise a specially shaped fore-arm that will help him to hold his gun with his damaged hand? Whatever ingenious stock modifications he invents, however, there is still no magic in a special gun or stock that will enable the handicapped shooter to shoot well unless he takes the trouble to retrain himself to do so.

The class of special stocks used by unhandicapped shooters for special purposes should be mentioned. The most common special features are those connected with trap-shooting: unusually long stocks, special grips such as the Etchen or thumb-hole, stocks without the usual notch at comb, or stocks with a specially curved or adjustable buttplate. Stocks that have been cut especially short for children, stocks cast or fitted with cheekpiece for a left-handed shooter, stocks with English comb measurements, or stocks set to any unusual measurements of cast, comb, or pitch for some individual or some special purpose, should be looked out for when considering the purchase a a second-hand gun. What may seem to be a bargain may only be the customary discount at which guns with unusual stocks are sold. The prospective purchaser should take into account the cost of remodeling or restocking such guns before buying. Unfortunately, the shooter who goes to the trouble of obtaining a special stock is often lowering the value of his gun.

13
Shotgun Sights and Ribs

Since the stock is so intimately concerned with shotgun sighting these subjects are reviewed here as an introduction to the procedure of sighting-in.

It is sometimes remarked in connection with the rapidity of the act of shooting that the shooter sees the rib or front sight only "subconsciously," and so might well dispense with one or the other. Few shooters do, however, and most feel that they are somehow helped by both these sighting devices. There are two pieces of physiological evidence that suggest shooters see the rib and front sight more than they think they do. They see them in a slightly different way than they may expect, however, because their perception is affected by what psychologists call the "gradient of clarity of the field of vision" and by the focus of the lens of the eye. Both principles are operative at the same time and both depend on the fact that the shooter's eye is fixed and focused, or should be, on the moving target.

The uneven clarity of the field of vision seen by the fixed or "fixated" eye must not be confused with the usual method of seeing, with the constantly moving eye, called "scanning," which gives the impression of uniform clarity of the field of vision. The concept of the gradient of clarity means that when the eye is fixated on a point, visual clarity is maximal at that point and decreases progressively from it toward the periphery of the field of vision.[61] The reader can easily verify this by keeping his eyes fixated on a random letter on this page. He will find that only the immediately surrounding words will be legible, the others progressively blurred toward the edge of the page. Thus, in pointing the gun, the shooter sees the target clearly in the center of his field of fixated vision, but sees the barrel or rib less distinctly because they are more peripheral.

The impossibility of simultaneously focusing on both near and far objects can be appreciated by simply trying to do so through a pair of binoculars. In aiming a rifle with open sights the rifleman focuses, like the shotgunner, on the target. He is long accustomed to the fact that he sees the front sight more clearly than the rear sight because, being farther away from the eye, it is more nearly in focus. In shooting the shotgun, although it has no rear sight, this same effect occurs. The front sight is seen with more clarity than the rib (or barrel) and the action (or receiver) which are perceived less distinctly because they are closer to the eye and farther out of focus.

This optical effect will increase as the shooter becomes older and finds himself noticing an increasing degree of far-sightedness (presbyopia). His far vision will be as acute as ever, while he will experience more difficulty in focusing on near objects until he eventually finds himself obliged to wear glasses for reading. This expected visual change will not ordinarily interfere with the shotgunner's shooting skill with the gun he has heretofore used. If he feels at some point that his perception of the front sight is less clear than he likes, he can have a more conspicuous front sight installed or use a gun with a longer eye-to-front-sight distance. Shooters who ordinarily wear corrective glasses for near-sightedness (myopia), astigmatism, sensitivity to bright light, or other reasons may prefer to have special large-field lenses for shooting. A shooter who has any reason to suspect that he is experiencing abnormal visual changes should consult a physician certified by the American Board of Ophthalmology, out of consideration for his own health and the safety of those he shoots with. Visual changes are often not what they seem until analyzed by a competent specialist, and may sometimes be symptoms of general rather than purely optical problems.

Shooters are usually advised to point the shotgun with both eyes open. This is theoretically sound because using two eyes (binocular vision) results in the ability to judge distance (depth perception), enlargement of the field of vision, and a considerable increase in the brightness of what is seen. The reality of these aspects of binocular vision and their tremendous advantage for the shotgunner can be grasped simply by looking at something within normal shotgun range with one eye closed and then opening that eye and looking with both eyes.

Unfortunately, while the advantage of shooting with two eyes open is easy to appreciate, doing it is difficult for some shooters. As with being right or left-handed, most people's vision is dominated by one eye or the other. Statistics seem to indicate that about one-third of right-handed people do not have complete ocular dominance on the right, and about one half of those who are left-handed do not have complete left ocular dominance. The written experience of practicing gunfitters, however, suggests that master eye problems

Shotgun Sights and Ribs

among shooters are very much rarer than this data would imply. Although most of the time eye dominance goes unnoticed, it can become apparent in situations demanding directed linear vision, such as sighting along a straight edge, or pointing a shotgun.

The classic test for ocular dominance is to look at a point with both eyes open and line up the tip of a finger between it and the eyes. If the alignment of the finger stays the same when the left eye is then closed, the right eye is dominant because it took charge and made the alignment when both eyes were open. If the left eye had been dominant when both eyes were open during alignment, the finger would appear to stay in the same place when the right eye was closed. If some change in alignment appears to take place when either eye is subsequently closed, eye dominance may be uncertain. A specialist's help may be desirable.

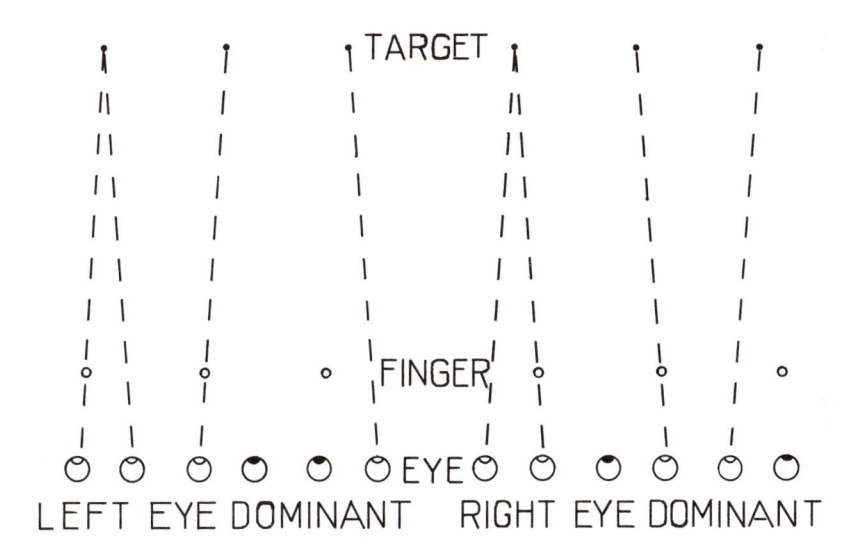

```
         ↑       ↑      ↑TARGET↑      ↑      ↑
         ‖       |      \      ‖      \      |
         ‖       |      \      ‖      \      |
         | \     |      \      | \    \      |
         | \     |      \      | \    \      |
         | \     |      \      | \    \      |
         | \     |      \      | \    \      |
         | \     |   o  \FINGER| \  o  \     | o
         | \     |      \      | \    \      |
         | \     |      \      | \    \      |
         o  o  o  o  o  oEYEo  o   o    o    o
       LEFT EYE DOMINANT     RIGHT EYE DOMINANT
```

When the shotgunner, whose dominant eye is really not on the same side as he shoulders his gun, tries to shoot with both eyes open he will align the target diagonally through the front sight across to the dominant eye on the off side, racking up a clean miss.

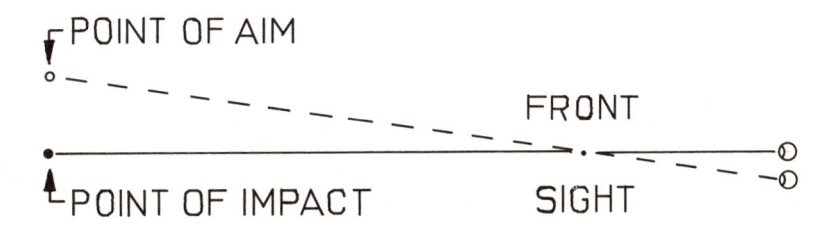

```
  ┌POINT OF AIM
  ↓
  o─ ─ ─ ─ ─ ─ ─ ─ ─ ─ ─ ─ ─
                                    FRONT
  •────────────────────────────•────────⊙
                                   ─ ─ ─⊙
  ↑POINT OF IMPACT           SIGHT
```

Most shooters who consciously or unconsciously have this problem have solved it by closing the off-eye (winking or "blinking") while shooting, thus pointing only with the eye on the side the gun is mounted even if it is not dominant. Shooting glasses that block the vision of the off-eye, a blinder-paddle attached to the side of the gun, or optical sights have been used by some shooters who have trouble blinking one eye during gun pointing. The use of the offset sights or ribs or stocks described in the chapter on special stocks may be ill-advised. Burrard[62] and Nichols[63] have written extensively about the dominant eye problem from personal experience. Both advise that a youngster be tested for eye dominance before he is taught to shoot so that he can learn to mount his gun to the shoulder on the side of the dominant eye to begin with, regardless of whether he is right- or left-handed. This approach correctly emphasizes the role of learning at an age when inflexible habits are not yet established. Older shooters with the dominant eye on the wrong side who have spent years blinking the dominant eye and hitting the target should probably not try to learn to shoot with both eyes open. Whatever the advantage, retraining is extremely difficult, as witness Nichols's account in his own case.

The relatively recent revival of interest in rib design, and in the top of the receiver as a rearward extension of the rib, reflects popular recognition of the importance to good gun pointing of the entire upper surface of the gun between the front sight and the shooter's eye. Its role in gun alignment is supplementary to that of the front sight, helping the shooter to point more rapidly by guiding his eye toward the front sight. A rib can also help correct any tendency to canting the gun by offering the shooter's eye-leveling instinct a flat horizontal surface to work with.

To begin at the beginning, nearest the shooter's eye, credit should be given to Nichols for emphasizing the importance of the near end of the receiver of the repeating shotgun as a large bold marker to start the eye in the right direction.[64] That even a small object near the eye can affect gun alignment will be recognized by those who have been disconcerted by the slightly off-center toplever of a new break-open gun. Many repeaters now have a matted groove that serves as a rearward extension of the rib along the top of the receiver—what Nichols calls an "eye-catcher notch."[65]

Before trying to examine the role of the rib or barrel(s) in shotgun pointing, the picture seen by the shotgunner should be recalled. Almost all shotguns are regulated so that the eye of the shooter must look obliquely down over the topline of the gun instead of parallel to it, because the correct line of sight passes higher over the action or receiver than over the front sight. The single sighting plane of over-and-under and repeating guns offers the eye a narrower, more pointer-like picture. The side-by-side offers a wider and more conspicuous one. Quicker and more accurate pointing has, rightly or wrongly, been claimed for either type of sight plane. The transition to the single sight plane shotgun may be more natural for riflemen.

With side-by-side guns, stocked with the splinter type fore-end and grasped by the barrels, the shooter's field of vision is obscured by his fingers and thumb sticking up along either side. Factory stocked single sight plane guns are usually equipped with fore-ends that help keep the shooter's fingers from blocking his view. This disadvantage in the conventional side-by-side guns can be eliminated by a properly designed beavertail fore-arm. At the muzzle, however, the side field of vision is invariably less obstructed in single sight plane guns. Side-by-side guns with the muzzle end of the rib depressed below the level of the barrels are particularly offensive in this respect. This situation can be greatly improved by installing Nichols's Bev-L-Blok front sight with the bead set on top of a small ramp (provided the comb of the stock is adjusted to compensate for the elevation of the front sight). Doubles already equipped with a high rib at the muzzle offer a better visual field at the end of the barrels. The wide sight plane of side-by-side guns offers the shooter's eye a broad horizontal plane, which is probably superior to that of single sight plane guns for gun leveling and correcting cant.

When it comes to speed of alignment, Nichols makes the claim that the fastest pointing can be done with what he calls the "bridge-gap" sighting line, his term for the line from the receiver to the front sight of a gun without a rib.[66] He believes that while the rib may be more precise than the bridge-gap arrangement, the bridge-gap facilitates quicker gun alignment. Some shooters who use them feel this effect is implemented by the bulge of a variable-choke device.

The functions of the rib are as a simplified guide line from the receiver to the front sight, and as an artificial horizon for the optical correction of cant. The shotgun rib is far from new, but the hollow and/or swamped types have nearly vanished and new types have appeared.

Ribs are now standard equipment on side-by-side and over-and-under guns, and a frequently picked up option on nearly all repeaters. Ventilated ribs, which were designed to minimize heat waves over hot barrels, are often seen on field guns because they are easier and cheaper to install. Solid ribs are more appropriate for field use because they collect no rust or dirt. The wide rib has maintained a place only at the traps, where unusually wide ribs are seen on guns used by some impressively successful competitors.

The Shotgun Stock

HIGH-FLAT
NARROW

HOLLOW

LOW-FLAT
WIDE

STRAIGHT-VENTILATED

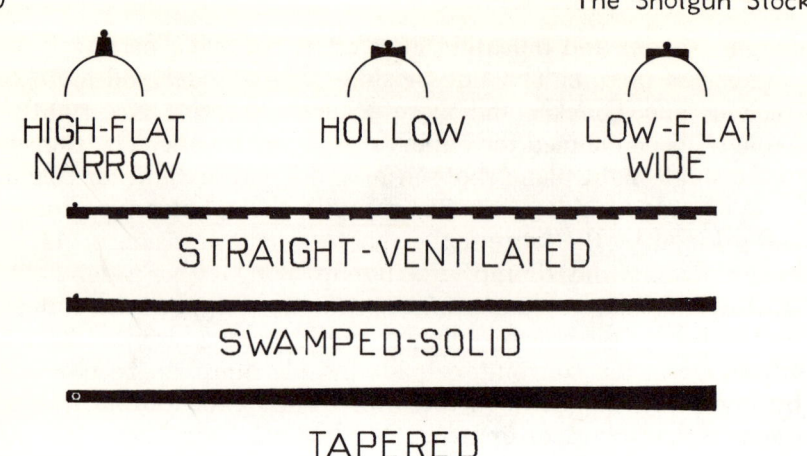

SWAMPED-SOLID

TAPERED

In general, modern field ribs are straight, flat, tend to be high and narrow, and are often tapered. These typical characteristics of present day design must be credited to Robert Churchill who introduced them on his "XXV" side-by-side gun. This rib was originally set high at the muzzle to lower the point of impact of such a short (25") barreled gun, and was narrow and tapered because this foreshortened perspective simulated the sight picture of the long-barreled gun then popular. The generally higher and narrower rib has probably resulted in a faster pointing gun, and has indirectly suppressed the use of a center sight in all but trap guns.

The surface of ribs is roughened by machining or filing in various designs, lumped together under the adjective *matted*. Matting is not the ideal solution to the problem of the visibility of the rib under impossible light conditions all too familiar to the upland or woods hunter, although it helps to eliminate glare when shooting in the sun in the clear. There have been a few speculative reports on light or conspicuously colored ribs.

The middle sight, located more or less halfway between the receiver and the front sight and much smaller (about $\frac{1}{16}$ inch in diameter) than the front sight, serves to correct cant and elevation. By breaking the flow of the rib it may increase pointing time. Its use has become restricted to long-barreled guns used where more deliberated aim is practicable.

Round or slightly egg-shaped front sights are on the market in white or yellow metal (or even half and half), or ivory. Red or orange translucent plastic cylinders (round as seen end-on by the shooter) are also available. Diameters between about ⅛ inch and about $\frac{11}{64}$ inch are offered. The most generally used is about ⅛ inch. Whether or not the round sight profile is the best choice, its use has probably resulted from its convenience to gunsmiths in installation

Shotgun Sights and Ribs

rather than from any particular desirability in gun pointing. When any change is made in the front sight as regards height, a compensatory adjustment should be made at the comb. With the Churchill-type rib, a smaller front sight is sometimes used on short-barreled guns to increase the perspective illusion of a longer sighting plane. The usefulness of any front sight at all on a gun fitted with a high narrow rib might be questioned aside from its role in elevating the gun's line of sight. From the standpoint of visibility, a larger rather than smaller front sight may be desirable. Sights made of conspicuous materials are all the better, Simmons (Glow Worm) and Ithaca (Raybar) offer translucent red or orange plastic front sights that deserve high marks for visibility when shooting against a dark background. That this type of sight has not yet been widely accepted may be due to shotgunners' traditional hostility toward radical innovations, as with the breech-loader, the choke, or short-barreled guns.

Something should probably be said about altogether different systems of shotgun sighting. Open rifle-type front and rear sights are usually furnished on guns that combine shotgun and rifle barrels. The rear sight may have a special setting or leaf, or may be turned down out of the way when the weapon is to be used as a shotgun. Low power or non-magnifying scopes are sometimes mounted on these combination guns, or occasionally on shotguns of any type. A comb that is fitted to accurately position the shooter's eye will facilitate the use of either of these sighting systems. Despite this, gun pointing takes longer than with the conventional system, additional time being consumed in finding the target through a scope, aligning a front and rear sight, or, in some cases, in turning down the latter. Within their limitations however, these systems have won and held a limited but secure place.

Another category of shotgun sights may be said to be truly optical in the sense that sight alignment does not require uniform positioning of the shooter's eye, so that fit at comb is not critical. One type (Nydar), employs the principle used in some aircraft gunsights. A new British sight (Singlepoint) is based on a collimator and requires binocular vision. In theory, sights in this classification might be brought to bear as quickly as conventional sights. They might then be expected to supplant them if testing by experienced shooters proved them superior in terms of hitting, perhaps because of increased luminosity or target visibility. The Nydar has failed to win general acceptance by American shooters, while British shooters have not had sufficient time to evaluate the Singlepoint.

Sights of whatever kind which profess to solve the problems of speed, angle, and distance in hitting flying targets are, of course, fakes.

14
The Ballistics of Shotgun Sighting

The purpose of this excursion into shotgun ballistics is to relate that peculiar subject to shotgun accuracy and the problem of sighting-in the shotgun. The shotgunner has a great many different factors to consider in choosing the ballistics that best suit his own type of shooting. Those that relate to shotgun sighting are the ones that control effective pattern diameter and the behavior of the pellets in flight. In discussing them it will be assumed that other ballistic factors are satisfactory for the shooter's purpose.

Test patterns are made by shooting against papers (American) or steel plates coated with non-drying paint (English). A *pattern* represents that portion of the total shot load that appears as a coherent circle of pellets in the judgment of the observer. This definable shotgun pattern consists of the total shot load less *flyers*—shot deformed enough to scatter in a completely irregular manner. Towards the outer edge of the definable pattern, except at very near range, the concentration of shot decreases to form a spotty ring or fringe that no longer contains enough pellets to be consistently effective against the target. It is the central *effective pattern* inside this fringe that concerns the shooter, whether for the sake of practical efficiency or sportsmanship.

Pattern diameter increases progressively with the distance of the pellets from the muzzle. The amount of increase is influenced by the choke of the barrel and the design of the ammunition regardless of gauge. The greater the degree of choke, the more the shot is concentrated toward the center of the pattern, and the smaller the diameter of the pattern. It has been customary to classify choke by a nomenclature running from *improved cylinder* through *full choke* or beyond, with the understanding that these adjectives mean a certain percentage of the shot pellets in a 30-inch circle at 40 yards. At present no such assumption can be made because of differences in choke construction between manufacturers. This confusion has been compounded by recent changes in ammunition design, which

The Ballistics of Shotgun Sighting

tend to reduce pattern size: crimp closure instead of end wads, shot cups and other devices that protect the shot from direct contact with the barrels; chilled, copper, or nickel plated shot; and, most recently, polyethylene buffered shot (Winchester-Westen HD).

A variable factor influencing shot concentration and pattern size is the difference in air resistance with changes in air density due to altitude or increased temperature. Boughan has documented a 20 percent increase in shot concentration between sea-level and an altitude of 7500 feet.[67]

TABLE NO. 1.   THE EFFECTIVE SHOTGUN PATTERN

Range (yds.)	Pattern Diameter (ins.)		
	Imp. Cyl.	Mod. Choke	Full Choke
10	15	12	9
15	18	15	12
20	20	16	14
25	26	22	18
30	30	26	22
35	36	32	28
40	44	40	36

The effective pattern diameters for the three most common choke designations are represented in Table No. 1. They are adapted from Burrard's figures because his work is widely accepted and because the concept of the effective pattern is his.[68] Shot size is not specified and these patterns were made with ammunition that did not have shot cups or crimp closures. The figures are averaged from many test firings. Older studies of repeatability showed very wide variation in pattern density from one shot to the next with the same cartridges in the same barrel. Present day ammunition is greatly improved in this respect. Oberfell and Thompson estimated only a + or —5 percent variation from their extensive firings.[69] In any case the interested shooter should check the pattern sizes produced by his own gun with the type of ammunition he uses.

Given the effective pattern to start with, how much distance the shotgunner can afford to spend on gun-pointing error is theoretically the distance between the center of the pattern and its outer edge: the radius of the circle of the effective pattern. This margin of error, which Burrard calls *the permissible error of aim*, is shown in Table No. 2 by range and choke.[70]

TABLE NO. 2.   THE PERMISSIBLE ERROR OF AIM.

Range (yds.)	Permissible Error of Aim (ins.)		
	Imp. Cyl.	Mod. Choke	Full Choke
10	7.5	6	4.5
15	9	7.5	6
20	10	8	7
25	13	11	9
30	15	13	11
35	18	16	14
40	22	20	18

While these allowances for error are true at the target, variations in the behavior of the shot load on the way to the target can have a considerable effect on the available margin for error. The shotgun's spread of pellets and short range have tended to obscure the fact that the principles of ballistics apply to it as well as to the rifle: shotgun pellets do shoot groups, have a curved trajectory, and are deflected by wind like any other projectiles.

Oberfell and Thompson, firing from a rest at bullseye pattern papers with an average commercial quality single-barreled shotgun equipped with a rear sight, determined the centers of a series of patterns. They found that their estimated centers consistently formed groups that averaged one inch in diameter for every five yards distance between the muzzle and the target over the normal shotgun range (for 90 percent of the shots in a given series, with 10 percent of pattern centers irregularly outside a group of this size).[71] For any given shot the deviation between the point of aim and the center of the pattern is, of course, a matter of chance. The difference between the centers of any two successive patterns may be zero or the full diameter of the group expected according to Oberfell and Thompson's rule. At 40 yards, for example, any two such patterns may be exactly centered or may be centered eight inches apart, and at 60 yards, 12 inches apart.

The shotgun not only shoots much poorer groups than the rifle, but the trajectory of shotgun pellets drops much faster. Shot drop is summarized in Table No. 3 for the sizes of shot that are generally used at a given range.

The Ballistics of Shotgun Sighting

TABLE NO. 3. SHOT DROP (MUZZLE VELOCITY 1330–1185 F.P.S.).

Range (yds.)	2 Shot	4 Shot	6 Shot	7½ Shot	9 Shot
	\multicolumn{5}{c}{Shot Drop (ins.)}				
40	2–3	3	3	3–4	4
60	7–8	8–9	9–10	10–11	12–13

The amount of drop decreases with higher velocities and larger shot sizes. Drop fortunately occurs in only one direction: down: Its influence on shotgun accuracy can be compensated for by sighting-in the shotgun with the load the shooter wishes to use at the average range he expects to shoot the gun. This is particularly important for guns intended for long range shooting.

The effect of wind deflection on the shotgun pattern is much greater than on the rifle bullet. The factors governing the pellets' behavior under various wind conditions have been reviewed recently by Labisky.[72] Wind direction can have many different relationships to the line of fire. In shooting horizontally or at a slight elevation, wind deflection will vary from maximal when the wind is at a right angle to the line of fire, to nothing when the wind is parallel to the line of fire. When shooting over head or near the vertical the deflection will always be maximal or nearly so. Up or down drafts may also enter the picture. Assuming that the wind is directly across the line of fire, physics dictates that deflection is inversely related to shot size (the larger the shot, the smaller the deflection), directly related to wind velocity (doubling the velocity doubles the deflection), and increases rapidly with increasing range. Muzzle velocity is a negligible factor. From Table No. 4 it can be seen that even moderate crossing winds can significantly alter the gun's point of impact.

TABLE NO. 4. CROSSING WIND DEFLECTION OF SHOT.

Range (yds.)	Wind Velocity (M.P.H.)	2 Shot	4 Shot	6 Shot	7½ Shot	9 Shot
		\multicolumn{5}{c}{Shot Deflection (ins.)}				
40	10	4	5	6	7	8
	20	9	10	12	14	16
60	10	10	11	13	15	18
	20	20	23	27	31	36

Shot stringing, while a ballistic phenomenon belonging exclusively to the shotgun, is not considered here because its practical effect depends largely on the direction of a moving target.[73] The effects of shot grouping, shot trajectory and wind deflection on the direction of the pellets in flight may not be significant, may work in different directions, or their individual or cumulative effect may result in a considerable reduction in the shooter's permissible error of aim.

If we make the unlikely assumption that the shooter aims perfectly, he could theoretically use up his entire permissible error of aim on "permissible error of eye position" in the form of *permissible error in fit at comb*. Let's go back to the figures for permissible error of aim at the target and see how they apply to fitting the shotgun comb by reversing them—that is, by translating the margin for error at the target into margin for error at the eye, which is the same as the closeness of the fit of the comb. By trigonometry, if a is Burrard's permissible error of aim, then a' is the "permissible error in eye position" (stock fit at the comb) by the formula

$$\text{tangent } \alpha = \frac{a}{b} = \frac{a'}{b'}$$

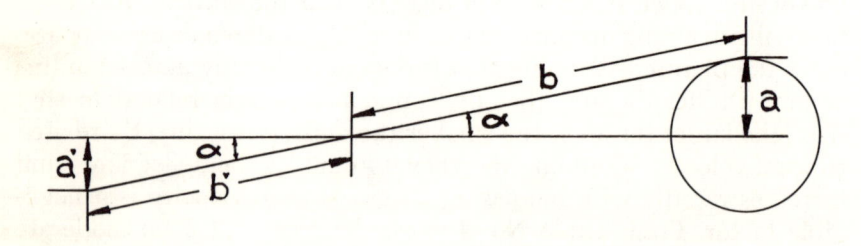

Table No. 5 shows the theoretical permissible error of fit at comb for the same three chokes and ranges used before and, to account for different sighting-plane lengths, for both a 26-inch barreled break-open gun with an eye to front sight distance of 34 inches and for a 28-inch-barreled repeater with an eye to front sight distance of 39 inches. The actual permissible error at the comb with perfect aim must be accepted as the minimum for any choke and sight plane, since the gun must be used throughout its range instead of only at its most favorable range from the standpoint of comb fit. It is a curious fact that the least advantageous ranges are also the most common. An examination of the figures shows at once the advantages offered by longer eye to front sight distance, and more open chokes.

The Ballistics of Shotgun Sighting

TABLE NO. 5. THEORETICAL PERMISSIBLE ERROR OF FIT AT COMB.

Range (yds.)	Eye-Front Sight (ins.)	Permissible Error (ins.) Imp. Cyl.	Mod. Choke	Full Choke
10	34	.71	.57	.43
10	39	.81	.65	.49
15	34	.57	.47	.38
15	39	.65	.54	.43
20	34	.47	.38	.33
20	39	.54	.43	.38
25	34	.49	.42	.34
25	39	.56	.48	.39
30	34	.47	.41	.35
30	39	.54	.47	.40
35	34	.49	.43	.38
35	39	.56	.50	.43
40	34	.52	.47	.43
40	39	.60	.54	.49

The shooter will also help himself by using ammunition that will not diminish the size of his gun's effective pattern, provided that the pattern remains dense enough with shot heavy enough to kill the game or break the target at the desired range. The shooter who uses modern commercial loads can expect that many of them will give a somewhat smaller pattern and less margin for error with a given choke than is indicated here.

We have already reviewed the factors affecting the flight of shot pellets on their way to the target that may reduce the shooter's margin for error. Inconsistency in cheek position and cheek pressure at the comb, however, are likely to reduce the margin for error considerably more than any other factors. The shooter cannot apply his cheek to the comb of the stock with exactly the same pressure every time he mounts his gun. And, as previously explained, if the shooter uses a stock whose comb has the conventional slope and taper, his eye will be displaced vertically or laterally if his cheek is displaced backwards or forwards. These sad facts can be easily verified by comparing the size of a pattern produced by firing a half dozen quick unrehearsed shots from different angles at a bullseye pattern with the size of a single pattern made at the same range.

Thus, some deduction must be made from the theoretical permissible error in fit at comb to allow for the variables of pattern and flight ballistics and error in gun mounting. There is not enough additional margin for error at the comb to compensate for poor fit and leave any margin left over to take care of error in gun pointing. The shooter needs all the help he can get from the closest possible fit at comb. The closer to perfection the better the shooter's chances, while only a little off perfection will make really good shooting impossible.

15
Sighting-In the Shotgun

The shotgun has a front sight; but unlike the rifle it has no rear sight to be lined up with it by eye. This is simply because the shotgunner doesn't have enough time to line up two sights before his bird is out of range. Since it has no visible rear sight, it is often said that the shooter "points" his shotgun instead of aiming it. He does, however, actually aim it, but without wasting time on a rear sight. He can do this with remarkable accuracy provided his eye is consistently positioned exactly as it would be if the shotgun really did have a rear sight. If it is, his eye is as good a rear sight as any, and much faster. It can be, if the comb fits him.

The main purpose of this section is to describe a procedure for fitting the comb to the shooter. However, the reason it is titled "sighting-in the shotgun" is that before the comb can be correctly fitted to the shooter, the accuracy of the gun itself must be checked out and a point of impact (pattern center) chosen for which the comb is to be fitted.

So far we have been talking about shotguns that can be correctly pointed. What about those with barrels that are defectively regulated so that correct pointing is impossible? This fault is not so rare as it should be and is not always consistent with the price of the gun. It should be checked for when purchasing any new shotgun, or attempting to fit the comb of any gun already owned. Three types of defective regulation can occur. Two-barreled guns, as we have seen, may not have the same point of impact for both barrels. Guns equipped with variable chokes may not have the same point of impact for different tubes or settings. Single barreled guns, or guns with two barrels that do shoot together, may have a single point of impact to the right or left of the point of aim. Combinations of these defects can, of course, also occur. Provided the points of impact are superimposed, and alignment is correct from side to side, the placement of the point of impact in the vertical plane is a matter of properly fitting the comb of the stock unless the point of impact is unusually high or low. A defectively regulated new gun should be rejected. Such a gun already in the shooter's possession should be disposed of or put in the hands of a very good gunsmith indeed.

The job of checking the point(s) of impact should be begun by improvising a temporary rear sight. A simple wooden open sight resembling those used on target pistols, which can be made with a file and a sharp knife or small chisel, is satisfactory.

It should be grooved or flanged on the bottom to accurately straddle the rib or fit the top of the receiver without wiggling when held in place by Scotch Tape or a wide rubber band. Any moderately hard wood that works cleanly can be used. Great care should be taken to center the sight notch and to make it the right size in relation to the front sight. At this stage in sighting-in the gun, the temporary rear sight should be somewhat higher than necessary (perhaps about $5/16''$). No effort need be made now to adjust it for elevation because it is desirable at this stage that the gun's point of impact be somewhat above the point of aim (about 6"-12"). Care must be taken to keep the sight mounted in the same position on the gun. Painting the sight with dark ink makes it easier to use.

Testing is done by aiming with the sight, without reference to the comb, with the aid of a rest at a large plain pattern paper marked with a small cross or bulleye. Shooting should be done in groups of enough rounds to produce a distinct picture. Single-barreled guns can be tested at the gun's expected average range. Two-barreled guns should be tested at the range the barrels are regulated to superimpose their pattern, usually 30-40 yards. All guns should center the pattern correctly from side to side in relation to the bullseye. If the gun has two barrels, both barrels can be aimed and fired alternately at the same paper until a definite pattern outline is made. Its shape and its size in comparison to that of a single pattern will determine if both barrels shoot together. The same procedure can be followed for guns with variable choke devices.

Provided point of impact testing is satisfactory, this is the time to evaluate the pattern quality (uniformity of shot distribution) of a new gun or an old one that has not been checked. Why and how is beyond the realm of this book, but any zealous shotgunner should

Sighting-In the Shotgun

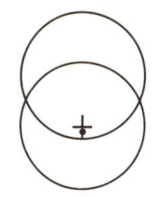

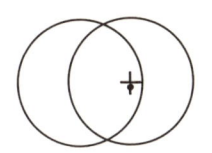

O/U BARRELS NOT TOGETHER

S/S BARRELS NOT TOGETHER

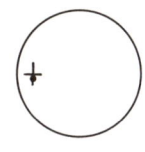

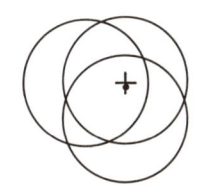

SINGLE BARREL SHOOTS TO RIGHT

VARIABLE CHOKE NOT TOGETHER

consult Oberfell and Thompson and do some form of pattern quality testing on any gun he thinks worth stocking well.[74]

When the shooter is satisfied with the gun's patterning quality he should then consider what is to be the relation between the top of the front sight and the center of the pattern at the average range at which the gun is to be used. The shooter has roughly three choices. He can center the pattern in line with the top of the front sight. He can center it a little higher, say a few inches above the top of the front sight, so that a bird that appears to "float" just above the sight will be centered in the pattern. Or he can deliberately set the pattern to center a good deal higher above the top of the front sight. The dead center arrangement has the advantage of pointing exactly on target, but considerably reduces target visibility. It may, however, be best for a gun intended for long-range shooting, as offering the most accurate sighting system for making allowances for wind, trajectory, and lead. The floating system, preferred by many hunters, improves visibility of the bird at little expense to accuracy. The gun set to shoot high by a considerable distance involves the shooter in the estimation of this distance in relation to the range and the size of the target, particularly difficult when ballistic and target speed calculations are also necessary. Its use is usually confined to shotgun games, including live pigeon shooting, where range, target size, and direction are known. In general the gun's point of impact should be set for the average range at which the gun is to be used. The shooter should take a realistic view of the distance at which his load will be effective against target or game. For reasons previously discussed in the section on balance and recoil it is important that he standardize on one load, or a narrow range of loads, when "setting his sights," and stick to it when fitting and shooting his gun.

Having chosen a point of impact the shooter can proceed with the next step in sighting-in the shotgun, which consists of adjusting the temporary rear sight slowly and carefully downward in the course of firing the gun at successive bullseye pattern papers. The final height of the temporary sight should be somewhat greater than that of the front sight (typical approximate measurements may be: front ⅛", rear ¼"). Adjustment should be made without reference to the existing comb, until the temporary sight centers the point of impact at the desired level. The end point height of the temporary sight is somewhat flexible provided it is not too low (an infrequent defect in regulation). If the shooter is lucky, a point may be found that offers the desired point of impact and at which the comb fit seems to be correct. If not, the comb must be adjusted to suit.

For this purpose the shooter is now in possession of a gun that is correctly sighted-in. The comb must be adjusted high, low, right, or left until it sets the shooter's eye in line with the temporary sight. Theoretically the practical job of shaping the comb so that the shooter's cheek is in the right position to line up his eye with the temporary rear sight is now easy. All the shooter would seem to need to do is to change the height and contour of the comb until his eye is always in the line of sight, without firing a shot. In practice, however, dry firing while fitting the comb must be extensively supplemented by real gun mounting during real shooting. Cheek position and cheek pressure are somehow different during dry-firing, and the fit of the comb must be checked by unrehearsed firing at the bullseye pattern paper from time to time without the temporary rear sight. Discrepancies, however, should be minor. If they are not, they may be due to inconsistencies in the shooter's style. As regards consistency, and without any foolhardy attempt to pontificate as to what is the right style, proper comb fitting can only be done by a shooter who has permanently adopted either a head-erect or head-down style of cheeking. A calculated and disciplined change in style of head position calls for refitting the comb. The shooter who does not consistently mount and cheek his gun in the same manner is wasting his time trying to fit the comb.

IV
STOCK DESIGN AND FIT

16
Shotgun Stock Design

The task of shotgun stock design is to join all the separate utilitarian parts of the stock to each other and to the metal gun to form a unit that is both practical and aesthetically pleasing. If shooters expect the whole gun to be as functional as a shovel and as handsome as a cock-pheasant, it is the problem of stock design to correlate the demands of utility and appearance. The art of stock design is to do this without comprising one or the other. Manufacturers sometimes sacrifice functional elements of the shotgun stock in order to keep down the cost of production and at the same time exaggerate some aspects of "styling" in order to compete for sales. This is just as ironic as paring costs by scrimping on good barrel regulation while featuring imitation "engraving." If any sacrifice need be made it should be the other way around, appearance giving way to function. Good stock design, regardless of the price of the gun, can make it unnecessary to choose between usefulness and good looks. The shooter should be able to have his cake and eat it too.

What the shooter expects from functional design isn't difficult to agree on: the stock should make it easy for him to carry the gun comfortably, mount it smoothly, point it accurately, and recover quickly from its recoil. Moreover, the stock should suit him as far as it contributes to the gun's weight and balance. Fortunately the functional aspects of a gunstock can be evaluated by the shooter in real terms. A given stock design either improves the gun's handling and shooting characteristics or not.

The principles underlying functional design have already been discussed in relation to each part of the stock. The purpose of this section is to discuss shotgun stock design from the standpoint of good looks. What makes a gun stocked in a certain way good looking may, of course, be dismissed by some shooters as a matter of personal or even national taste. However, it seems more constructive to take the position that certain gunstocks are generally regarded as classics, and to analyze them in the hope of understanding why these stock designs seem handsomer than others.

Before starting to consider some such designs, a distinction should be made between stock design and stock decoration. As regards appearance, design conventionally means the shape and lines of the stock as seen from the side. Decoration is the icing on the cake—carving, inlays, checkering layout, and the figure of the wood—topics which will be considered separately.

Any effort to design a shotgun stock has to start with the metal gun it is intended for. The shape given each type of shotgun by its action and barrel arrangement poses a different problem, so that there can be no universal stock design. If a gun type in general imposes design conditions, individual guns within a type may make it easy or difficult for the stock designer. Some mechanically very efficient guns have suffered from an apparent lack of coordination between engineer and stocker during the period of development. Given a metal gun that is not hopelessly ugly, a stock design can be fairly judged only as to whether or not it has made the most handsome marriage possible between wood and metal. The question of what gun or stock design is absolutely the best looking should be dropped to begin with by admitting that many different gun and stock designs can be attractive.

The side-by-side is often considered the most beautiful of all guns, probably because of its low slender profile, possible only with this barrel arrangement and the box- or side-lock, or the sliding breech action. Figures 13 and 14 show four different ways of stocking this metal gun. The traditionalist may sincerely have only one stock in mind for this gun: the straight grip and splinter fore-end. This style, older than the two-piece stocks of the earliest hinged-action breech-loaders, is derived from the one-piece stocks of Continental and English flint-locks nearly as old as "shooting flying." Most generally admired is the look of its straight grip buttstock which has an unbroken line from toe to action. The top and bottom lines of this grip are happily parallel to each other, while a projection of the line of the comb seems to converge exactly on the top of the action. The action itself appears to continue these lines forward so that the straight-grip buttstock has a slim, sleek look no version of the pistol-grip can match.

One straight-grip stock is illustrated with a splinter fore-end and one with a beavertail fore-end. Which of these is better looking may be subject to analysis. If it is granted that the fluid uninterrupted lines of the straight grip buttstock are particularly attractive because they form an elegantly elongated triangle with the

Fig. 13
The text attempts to analyze and compare the stocks of these straight-grip guns with each other and those in Fig. 14. At top is an inexpensive modern Italian version of the classic English game gun with splinter fore-end; at bottom, a Parker with beavertail fore-end. (Diehl's, Coll. Dr. Robert C. Snavely)

Fig. 14
Two side-by-side guns, both stocked with a pistol grip; one with a splinter fore-end, the other with a beavertail. **Top,** Parker. **Bottom,** inexpensive Spanish side-lock stocked for the American trade. The relationship between the pistol grip and different actions and fore-end designs is commented on in the text. (Coll. Dr. Robert C. Snavely, Diehl's)

Shotgun Stock Design

gun's action then it becomes possible to decide between the relative merits of either fore-end by the same standards. Seen in this light, the beavertail fore-end contributes more to the appearance of the gun because its straighter lines continue the same effect in relation to the barrels. The short splinter gives the gun a stubbier look and introduces a curve that has no relation to the rest of the gun or stock design.

Pistol grips interrupt the clean lower line of the buttstock with curves which may vary from a shallow arc to a pronounced "c." The stock designer who aims for good looks will have a hard time with the more extreme grips (Fig. 35, Bottom). With those more moderately curved, the success of his stock design will depend on how well the curved lines of the grip is related to curved lines on the fore-arm and the action of the gun. The two pistol-grip stocked side-by-side guns illustrated exemplify different relationships between the grip, and the action and the fore-arm. The Parker with the splinter fore-end seems to come off best in the fore-arm department, because its curved line echoes that of the grip, giving this gun the most symmetrical look. The reason the beavertail fore-arm has been more acclaimed for its practical advantages than for its looks is apparent in the case of the Spanish side-lock. Its nearly straight lines offer nothing to complement the curve of the pistol grip, giving the gun an unbalanced look.

A more harmonious relationship between the beavertail fore-arm and the pistol grip can be achieved by using the Schnabel type of fore-end (Fig. 43, Bottom). This style, characterized by a downward curve at the tip of the beavertail which pleasingly counterbalances that of the grip, has fallen into neglect since the demise of the old L. C. Smith firm which used it so effectively. When it comes to the relationship between the pistol grip and the action, the side-lock wins easily because the arc of the grip repeats the loop of the lock plate. As evidence, notice that the designer of the Parker stock felt it necessary to compensate for the absence of a lock-plate by adding a carved and checkered wooden plaque at the rear of its box lock action.

The challenge of designing stocks that make the most of other types of actions has not always been successfully met. However, in the context of the relationship between the pistol grip and the action, there are at least two examples that are classics in their own right (Fig. 15). They are particularly interesting because each has utilized a differently curved pistol grip to correspond to the clean curve of the upper line of its action. The Darne sliding-breech gun is not only outstanding in this respect but, by repeating this curve in its fore-arm and by rounding the cap of its pistol grip, achieves

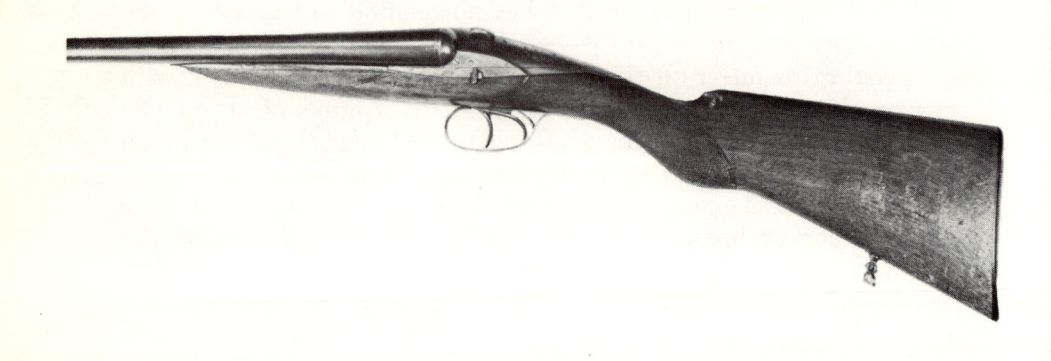

Fig. 15
Top, This very plainly stocked, much used Darne nevertheless shows the beautifully counter-balanced curves of fore-end, action, and grip that make it one of the most handsome stock designs.
Bottom, Even its unfortunate checkering layout can't obscure the elegant curve continuing from the back of the receiver through the pistol grip of this Winchester Model 12. (Mr. George Lyon)

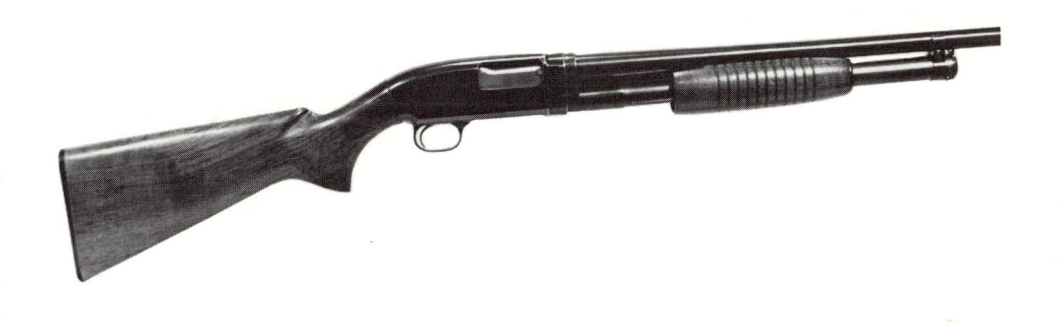

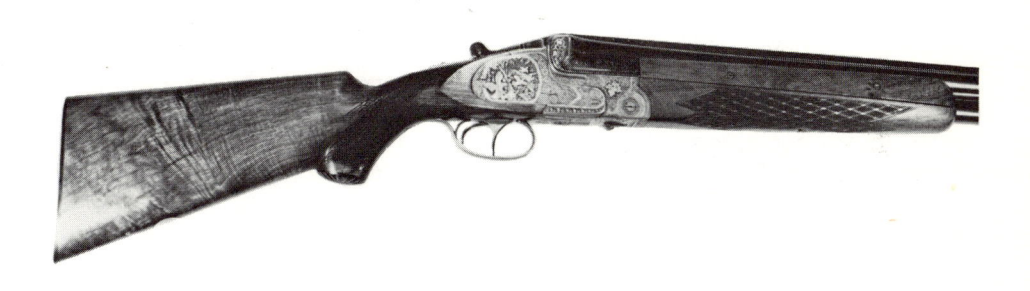

Shotgun Stock Design 101

Fig. 16
These two guns, both mechanically excellent, are commented on in the text because they illustrate some of the problems of stock design. **Top,** Winchester Model 12 with field grade stock. **Bottom,** Middle-European over-and-under.

a remarkable overall unity of design. In a newer type of gun, the single barreled repeater with its wide variety of actions, it is possible to see the evolution of its stock design. The continuous curve of the present custom Winchester Model 12 pistol grip and action is undoubtedly the correct one for this gun. It has not always been available, having evolved from the awkward grip used on earlier models of the same gun (Fig. 16, Top).

A comparison of these two Model 12 stocks serves to introduce another aspect of stock design that is particularly applicable to the class of repeater shotguns, and to a lesser extent to over-and-under guns. Both types have greater depth of action, and by reason of their magazine or barrel arrangement greater depth forward of the action, than do side-by-side guns. The profile of the side-by-side appears as a long slender triangle which is the basis of its best stock designs. The thicker profile of repeater and over-and-under guns requires a stock design that gives an appearance of scale and proportion between the fore and rear parts of the gun. The field grade Model 12, while not its best possible design, does achieve this balance by combining a light-looking sloping stock with a rather small handle fore-end (Fig. 16, Top).

The buttstock of the Custom Model 12 with its high comb for trap shooting appears heavier than that of the field grade. The designer has correctly compensated for this by thickening and elongating its fore-end so that it appears large enough to balance the gun's larger buttstock (Fig. 15, Bottom). To confirm this argument in regard to scale, the reader is invited to compare the photograph of a nameless over-and-under (Fig. 16, Bottom) with those of two well-balanced but differently stocked versions of the Browning over-and-under (Fig. 20). The anonymous gun appears awkwardly disproportionate as much because its buttstock is too slender and too sloping as because its fore-end is too long and too deep.

The early German-American rifle stock detrimentally influenced nineteenth-century American shotgun stock design. Currently the rifle stock seems to be having its second round at our shotgun stock. Features such as the sharply curved pistol grip with a wide flaring base, the roll-over comb, and the thumb-hole grip, intended for rifle-shooting, are being offered on shotgun stocks for both trap and field guns by some commercial stockers (Fig. 17). All would seem to be a definite hindrance to either carrying or mounting a shotgun in the field, so that their use in field stocks should be condemned. Since the trap gun forms a special category because its stock need not meet field requirements, trap shooters are certainly free to evaluate the merits of these rifle stock innovations in their sport. If they come to be generally adopted, stockers will have the

Shotgun Stock Design   103

Fig. 17
This left-handed rifle stock is shown less for its remarkably fine and uniform stump-figure walnut, than to indicate the degree to which the contemporary American rifle stock has influenced some recent shotgun stock designs. Variations of this "roll-over" Monte Carlo comb, and the exaggerated flare at the end of the pistol grip, are now offered for shotguns by several commercial restockers. (Flaig's)

problem of incorporating them into good looking designs.

In the history of shotgun stock design a great many years were consumed in arriving at the finest stock designs for the side-by-side gun. No sooner had these styles been established than new metal gun types appeared. The invention of the family of American repeating guns together with a revival of interest in the over-and-under gun presented entirely new problems in stocking. Only a few of the new types lasted in one form long enough for designers to give serious consideration to the best way to stock them. At present the flow of radical shotgun innovations seems to have paused so that shotgun stockers can find time to ponder ways of improving stock design for existing gun types. The trend toward the application of purely rifle stock elements to the field shotgun or the use of sales-oriented mannerisms which may be called "sculptured styling" may well last until painstakingly thought-out formulas for stocking different new gun types achieve the best possible combination of good looks with sound functional qualities.

Something really new in stock design is unlikely. Everything has probably been tried by some stockmaker, somewhere, sometime. But the best that can be done with all the possibilities of stock design has rarely been realized. Any sound development in stock design should be based on the practical aspects of the stock. Improving hand-holds, a return to less sloping combs, or the adaptation of the line-of-sight comb to field stocks may offer the greatest opportunities for functional improvement in the stock today. The challenge is to incorporate such features into stocks with really handsome lines. Under present conditions commercial stockmakers and gun manufacturers will tend to be preoccupied with production costs and sales promotion. Better designs will have to come from those most devoted to the shotgun: the shooters themselves, and the small gunsmiths and stockmakers who are deeply interested and thoroughly experienced in shooting and have the time for experimental work.

17
Fitting the Shotgun Stock

Personal stock measurements are sometimes quoted in a way that gives the impression that they are magic numbers which, once determined for one gun, can be used to correctly fit the shooter for any gun he ever acquires. Unfortunately, this is far from true because so many variables enter into the problem of fitting a particular gun. Variable factors influencing the individual's stock measurements can be divided into three classes: those depending on the shooter's physique and shooting style, those related to gun design and performance, and those that are related to special conditions or are simply optional. The influence of these factors has been discussed in detail previously and will not be repeated here to elaborate a point, but some generalizations are worth making.

The shooter often mistakenly tends to think of his physical self as a constant because he is unaware of the slow changes it undergoes as he grows and ages. He changes in stature, strength and endurance; his reflexes sharpen or dull, and his ability to concentrate waxes and wanes. These metamorphoses must be balanced against the shooter's accumulation of experience: his ability to analyze and improve his shooting style or not. His preference in guns and the type of shooting he does will probably change too. He will need different stock fitting to suit these changes, and he may want to try different stock designs, and tinker with gun weight and balance.

Some of the parts of the stock are difficult or impossible to specify by measurement at all. This is particularly true of curved lines, tapers, cross-sections, irregularly contoured areas such as handholds, cheekpieces, undercuts; and the factors that affect gun balance. A change in one part of a stock will often change the measurements of others because the measurements of many different parts of the stock have a reciprocal relationship. For instance, if we assume that the shooter actually places his cheek at one certain point on a sloping comb above which his eye is in the correct line of sight, drop-at-comb and drop-at-heel must be changed reciprocally in order to maintain the identical eye-to-comb distance.

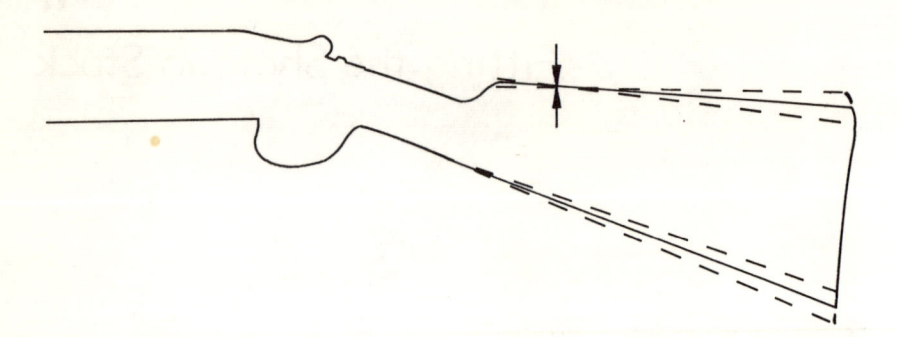

Another example is the relationship between the comb and stock length. If the stock is shortened or lengthened, the shooter's cheek will be displaced forward or backward along the comb, so that his eye will be displaced up or down in relation to the true line-of-sight.

How far can methods of measurement of the shooter himself help in fitting the stock to him? In discussing the parts of the stock the parameters of stock dimensions and the principles involved in fitting have been discussed. Methods have been suggested for fitting some aspects of the stock by measurement of the shooter. Unfortunately, however, he can only be accurately measured for cast-at-toe and to some extent for fitting the butt. In addition a procedure has been outlined for sighting-in the shotgun and fitting the comb that involves both precision and trial and error. Fitting the other parts of the stock remains essentially a trial and error business. And even the fit of those parts of the stock amenable to measurement must be confirmed by practical testing. While the importance of fitting the shotgun stock to the shooter has been widely acknowledged, the fact that fitting is so largely a matter of trial and error has prevented many shotgunners from having properly fitted guns.

This situation was recognized by the British in developing the try-gun and the professional gun fitter (Fig. 18). The try-gun can be adjusted for fitting length, cast, pitch, and the height and slope of the comb, but lacks any means for testing the size or fit of the grip, undercut, butt, fore-arm, or the contour of the comb. Fitting is done by an experienced technician using the facilities of a shooting grounds or school. A recent description of the procedure tallies with others in the literature, suggesting that it is fairly well standardized.[75]

The fitter first evaluates the shooter, makes preliminary settings

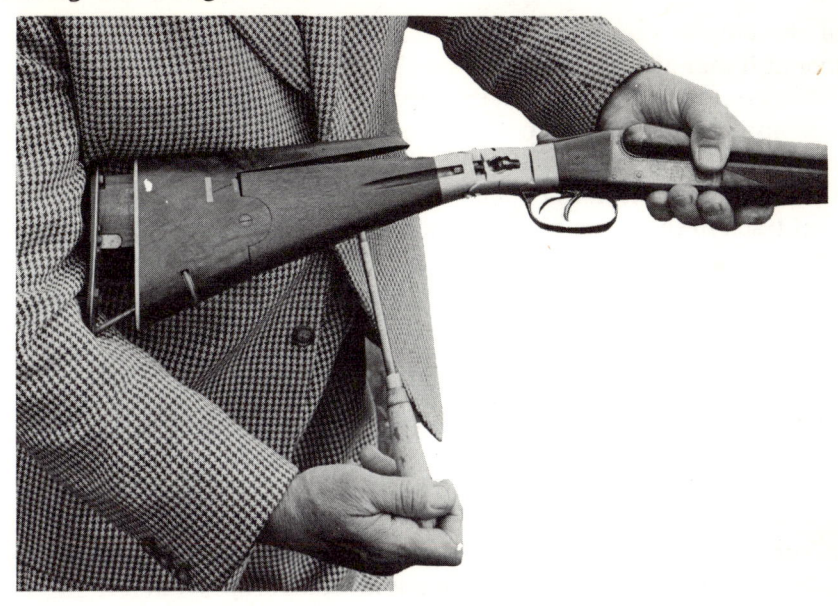

Fitting the Shotgun Stock 107

Fig. 18
This try-gun used by one of the great surviving London makers of "best" guns, Holland and Holland, is shown being adjusted and measured. Note their practice of measuring drop at comb at a point behind that in general use. (Holland and Holland, Ltd., London)

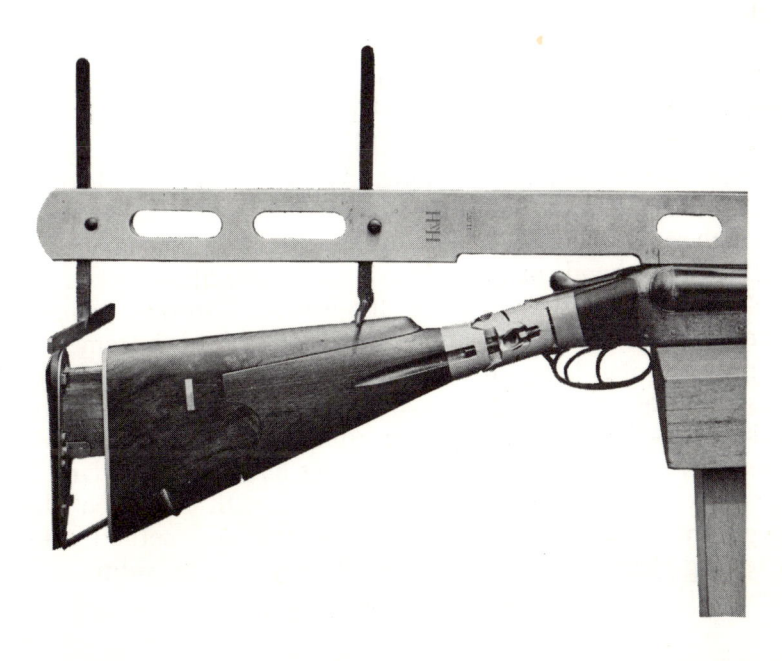

of the empty gun, and then adjusts it after observing the shooter mount it and aim at the fitter's eye. The next step consists of rapidly firing groups of shots at a stationary target. After the gun has been readjusted to center the pattern correctly at a still target, it is then used against clay pigeons thrown to simulate a variety of game shots. Correcting gun fit here depends on the fitter's skill in observing the shot track in the air as he stands behind the shooter. The last stage is said to be a final fitting of the gun "in the white" (before metal browning or blueing and stock finishing).

The procedure is undoubtedly basically sound because it recognizes and solves much of the trial and error problem in fitting. Criticism of the try-gun may be directed toward its method of employment and the people involved. It should be understood first of all that this type of fitting is at its best in the hands of the personnel of English "best" gun makers who offer only a limited range of gun and stock types. For reasons already developed, the dimensions of a correct fit with a side-by-side try-gun cannot be translated in terms of the multiplicity of gun and stock types offered in the United States. Such authorities as Burrard have complained of poor fit and the lack of uniform results among different fitters.[76] Certainly the shooter is at the mercy of the fitter, but the fitter might well complain of insufficient time and incompetent shooters. All practitioners who have written about fitting have regarded it as futile in the case of unformed, inconsistent shooters. The possibility of errors of self-deception, or a change of style or timing under unfamiliar circumstances, may be real even in the case of experienced shooters.

At any rate the British try-gun and expert fitter system, for better or worse, is available in the United States only in the person of traveling representatives of British "best" gun makers but without comparable shooting facilities. While a number of try-guns exist in the hands of American manufacturers or dealers, at least one of these is not used in a manner to achieve the quality of fit possible in the hands of the professional British fitter.

No American system of fitting has evolved. However, since trial and error is unavoidable, the idea of a try-gun is an extremely good one provided it is adapted to the gun to be fitted and can actually be used thoroughly enough to make sure that the gun really does fit the shooter. For lack of anything comparable to the professional British system, American shotgun fitting has depended largely on the efforts of shooters to fit their own stocks with or without the aid of a gunsmith. Stock remodeling has been the only method available for testing changes in the gunstock. Remodeling by subtraction, as in converting from a pistol to a straight grip, shortening the stock,

Fitting the Shotgun Stock

or lowering the comb is a satisfactory but limited affair. Remodeling by addition means adding wood and then shaping by subtraction. Both methods are slow, irrevocable, and necessarily limited to parts of the stock where wood can safely be subtracted or added; they rule out changes at the grip and the fore-arm of many guns. Remodeling thus lacks the flexibility of the adjustable try stock, and shares its fault that not all aspects of stock size or fit can be tested by it.

Ideally a perfect try-stock should be easily adjustable in every dimension so that any part of the stock could be changed in any way and tested. The author proposes that the shooter meet these requirements by using his own gun as a try-gun.[77] By gradually rebuilding the existing stock into a durable working "try-stock" by the method to be described, the shooter can "try" his own gun by shooting until he is satisfied with its design and fit. Two such try-stocks can be seen in Figures 21-25. The completed and test-proven working try-stock can be sent to a stockmaker for reproduction by hand or, more cheaply, by the highly accurate duplicating machines used by the better-equipped commercial stockmakers (Fig. 19).

Buying a blank and correctly fitting it to the gun is beyond the scope of this book because of the jigs, tools, and experience involved. Books on gunsmithing contain methods to which the reader may refer.[78] The shooter who simply wants to remodel his present stock may still benefit by the try-stock procedure. This decision must be made in advance and the try-stock prepared within the limitations of remodeling. Remodeling will be discussed at the end of this section.

Preparation of the try-stock itself requires very little expense in tools or materials and a minimum of woodworking skill. The tools needed for reshaping or removing wood are simple flat, rounded, or round woodworking rasps and files, and perhaps one or two small gouge-type chisels if their use is familiar, plus sandpaper of different grades and a sandpaper block. Building up parts of the try-stock can be done by glueing on successive flexible layers of $\frac{1}{32}$ inch balsa wood (from stores that sell model making supplies), or straight-grained veneers (available through planing mills), or by building up layers of Plastic Wood applied in about the same thickness. Other materials, such as gun bedding preparations or the synthetics used for boat repair might possibly be used in thick applications. The author has not tried them. Given equal durability the material itself is of little importance.

While a single application would be faster, there is much to be said for the slow thoughtful build-up of thinner layers. Several layers of balsa or veneer can be glued on at one time and held in position by bandaging them tightly to the stock by wrapping them

Fig. 19
The duplicating machine makes it possible for the operator to cut copies to remarkably close tolerances by tracing a master stock, seen at center here, (or the shooter's own try-stock). Competent professional stockers also have the tools, jigs, and experience to do accurate inletting work. The shooter can choose a blank of a weight and quality to suit him, and end up with his personally designed and fitted stock at reasonable cost. (Flaig's)

on with an elastic ("Ace") bandage fastened with small clips. Plastic Wood will not dry in depth, so the layers must be kept thin and each layer completely dried before the next is applied. The existing surface of the stock should be roughened before applying balsa, veneer, or Plastic Wood in order to ensure good adhesion. No attempt should be made to produce an even surface between successive layers of Plastic Wood so that the next layer will adhere better. Blocks of an easily worked wood such as white pine can be glued on to extend the butt. They are easily held in place by an Ace bandage secured through the trigger guard.

Shaping the try-stock should always be performed under a bright

Fitting the Shotgun Stock

raking light, that is: the light source should be above and on the far side of the work so that it casts a shadow on it, down and toward the operator's eye to help him see any imperfections. If the try-stock is carried to the stage of complete surface smoothness needed for machine-duplication, it helps to keep it painted with a water-based fast drying paint, such as Liquitex (available at art supply stores), in some neutral color so that it is easier to detect slight irregularities in the surface. Care must be taken not to damage the stock inletting or metal parts of the gun. Padding should be kept between the wood or metal and any clamp or vise, and the action kept clean of debris and abrasive dust before reassembling for testing and measuring. Try-stocks so constructed hold up perfectly well during shooting, and can be test-fired or used in the field almost indefinitely if they are waterproofed.

In making a try-stock the shooter has the advantage over both the English try-gun and remodeling. He is able to work on any part of the stock and is free to add or subtract material back and forth at will. With something like the freedom of a sculptor working with clay, the shooter can try design ideas and change them in the course of fitting and testing the stock. He must, however, work within the limitations of the metal gun, paying attention to straps, tangs, trigger-guards, and fore-arm attachments. No great woodworking experience is necessary if the try-stock work is carefully thought out and cautiously done. The thing is to do more looking and measuring than working. Remove material slowly or add it thoughtfully, and continuously test the stock's fit. Attempts at craftsmanship and finish until the end of the job may be a liability by distracting the shooter from concentrating on stock design and fit.

The shooter should have a clear idea to begin with of what he wants to do, whether it is simply to improve the fit of the comb, or redesign and fit every part of the stock. Before any extensive changes are made he should thoroughly familiarize himself with the alternative possibilities available for each part of the gunstock as well as its overall design, and develop some concept of the kind of new stock he expects to have. He should be sure in advance that the metal structure of the gun permits such changes. He should also have some idea what practical improvements he can expect these changes to contribute to handling and shooting the gun. What seems theoretically correct or looks good is often wrong in practice. The gun should be fired as much as possible during this planning period as well as during actual fitting while the try-stock is in process. A critical analysis of the shortcomings of the old stock can prevent the shooter from getting a new stock as bad or worse. The old stock should be measured, and the figures kept for reference.

Actual work should proceed in a sequence that brings each change in the stock to a usable state of completion in turn so that the gun can be fired and one change evaluated before proceeding with another. Each change should be assessed according to what it is intended to do. Changes in the comb, for example, in terms of point of impact; changes in the butt in terms of gun-mounting; or changes in hand-holds literally in terms of the feeling of a good hold on the gun. Since the chapter on experimental shotgun stocks contains a blow-by-blow description of the redesigning and fitting of two basically different types of shotgun stocks, the work sequence will only be outlined here.

The logical place to begin is with any changes to be made at the butt. Problems of stock length, drop-at-heel, cast, butt dimensions, and pitch must all be resolved before the shooter can be expected to position his cheek (and eye) consistently at the comb. The buttplate or recoil pad to be used should be selected in advance, so that its thickness and shape are known factors. An appropriately shaped temporary wooden substitute may be useful for trial and error fitting. It is important (especially with a cast stock) to mark the butt and the comb for their true center lines.

When changes at the butt have been completed, fit at comb can be set (with the aid of the temporary rear sight). The contour of the body of the stock next to the shooter's cheek, or a cheekpiece, should be fitted at the same time as the comb. Fitting the grip and fore-arm and body of the stock follow. When the gun is assembled and try-stock fit is tested at the work bench, the shooter should remember to do so in a standing position as he normally would when handling and shooting the gun.

Lastly the parts of the stock can be tied together as pleasingly as possible. If all the functional parts of the stock are brought into a usable state without fine finishing, fit and design can be refined in the course of as much field testing as the shooter wants. Between the knowledge acquired from working with and thinking about the gun and its stock, and the reward of having a really well fitted gun, many devoted shotgun men will think their time well spent. If the completed try-stock is to be put in the hands of a professional stockmaker for copying, the shooter who expects to ever see his gun again cannot make arrangements too far in advance.

The possibilities of remodeling should not be neglected. The principle of remodeling is to use the existing stock as a skeleton, subtract or add wood, and reshape it to the proper fit. It may offer an economical method of doing limited stock fitting. Remodeling by subtraction, mentioned earlier, is certainly simple. Remodeling by addition is more demanding and tedious, and can be expensive un-

Fitting the Shotgun Stock   113

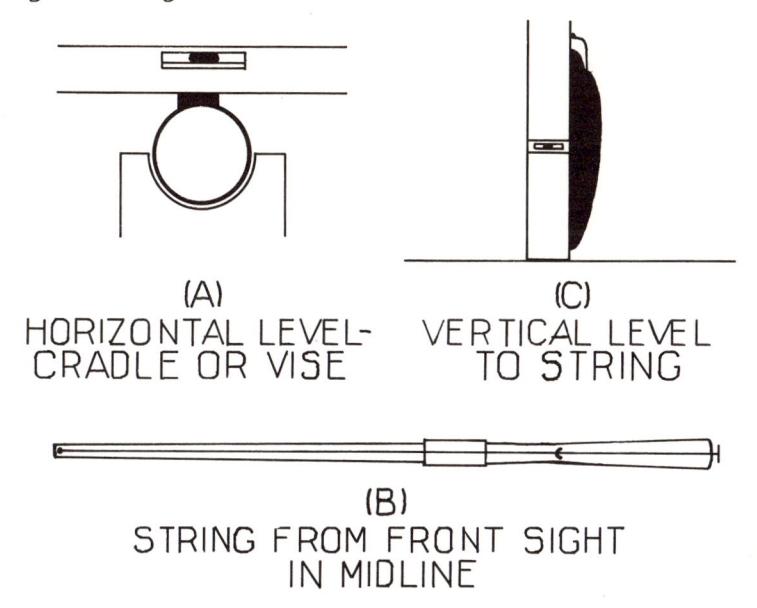

(A)
HORIZONTAL LEVEL-
CRADLE OR VISE

(C)
VERTICAL LEVEL
TO STRING

(B)
STRING FROM FRONT SIGHT
IN MIDLINE

less the shooter is skillful enough to do it himself.

The existing stock can be made into a try-stock and then used as the "frame" for remodeling. All possible patterns, photographs, and measurements should be taken before the try-stock is dismantled. Additions to the try-stock must be limited to those that are feasible as wooden additions later. Careful advance planning of where and how much wood to apply is extremely important. Adding more wood and to a larger surface than the minimum expected to be necessary for the finished stock will prevent mistakes. The wood used in remodeling should be as much like that of the existing stock as possible. Close matching of figure and texture and keeping the grain of the attached blocks running in the same direction as the wood of the stock is not difficult with most straight-grained commercial stocks and greatly improves the appearance of the end result (Fig. 10). If the stock is to be lengthened, an access channel must be left open in the butt if the stock is attached by a draw-bolt. Attention must be paid to any hollowing in the buttstock and to the location of whatever is inside the fore-arm.

Preparing the old stock consists of planing perfectly flat areas onto its surface where equally flat areas of new blocks of wood are to be glued. The preparation of the surfaces necessary for glueing is easy and simple with woodworking machines and difficult with hand tools even for the accomplished woodworker. The shooter who does not have experience with planing and shaping tools should have this work done (under his eye) by someone who does, perhaps a cabinet maker at a local planing mill. If the surfaces are exactly matched, and the wood applied is as strong as the original stock wood, no damage at all will be done to the structural soundness of the stock provided a suitable glue is applied evenly between them and they are clamped together with even pressure long enough for complete curing.

An increasing number of synthetic adhesives is available, differing in durability, color, moisture resistance, and preparation and curing factors. Their advantages and disadvantages have recently been reviewed from the stockmaker's standpoint.[79] Small short dowels fitted between the two pieces will help prevent slipping when the clamps are applied. The use of moderately dark staining before the application of the finish can produce a good-looking stock that may show very little evidence of remodeling. The work of shaping the stock can only be satisfactorily done by hand tools, as previously described.

However, since the main consideration in remodeling is economy the shooter might have as sound a stock, a cheaper one, and certainly a better fitted one if he simply completed a try-stock (prepared without the limitations imposed by remodeling), stained it dark, and finished it like any other gunstock. In this case balsa wood should not be used.

18
Experimental Shotgun Stocks

While most of the emphasis of this book has been on the importance of properly fitting the shotgun stock to the individual shooter and how to do it, a good deal of material has also been presented on the possibilities of the different elements of shotgun stock design. The combination of special design features with individual fitting using the try-stock method offers the shotgunner an opportunity to create stocks adapted to his own ideas as well as to his own fit.

He can experiment with each part of the stock, test its performance by shooting the gun until he is certain that its design and fit are practical, and then tie these proven parts together in a way he thinks is good looking. When individual fit is seriously undertaken by the shooter on his own behalf, and he designs and tests the parts of the gunstock for himself, it is surprising how often the functional stock that results is more handsome than those designed primarily for looks. Even the most expensive gun cannot be as thoroughly fitted by the most careful gun-maker and the stocks of such guns all look alike. The shooter's own design will be his very own baby—and a pleasure to have and shoot—that he cannot buy.

The two guns illustrated present different stocking problems and different solutions, but by no means the only problems or the only solutions. One is a light-weight, short-barreled, straight-hand grip over-and-under for fast upland shooting with moderate 12-gauge loads (Figs. 20-22). The general problem, aside from fitting, was to convert it to a line-of-sight comb and to design grip and fore-arm hand-holds contoured to the shooter for quick, consistent mounting and pointing. The other gun is a heavy, longer-barreled, pistol-grip and recoil-pad equipped semi-automatic used for stationary long range shooting with maximum 12-gauge 3-inch loads (Figs. 23-25). The problem was to fit and redesign this efficient but somewhat awkward and homely gun for the best possible gun control and pointing quality and to try to improve its general appearance. A

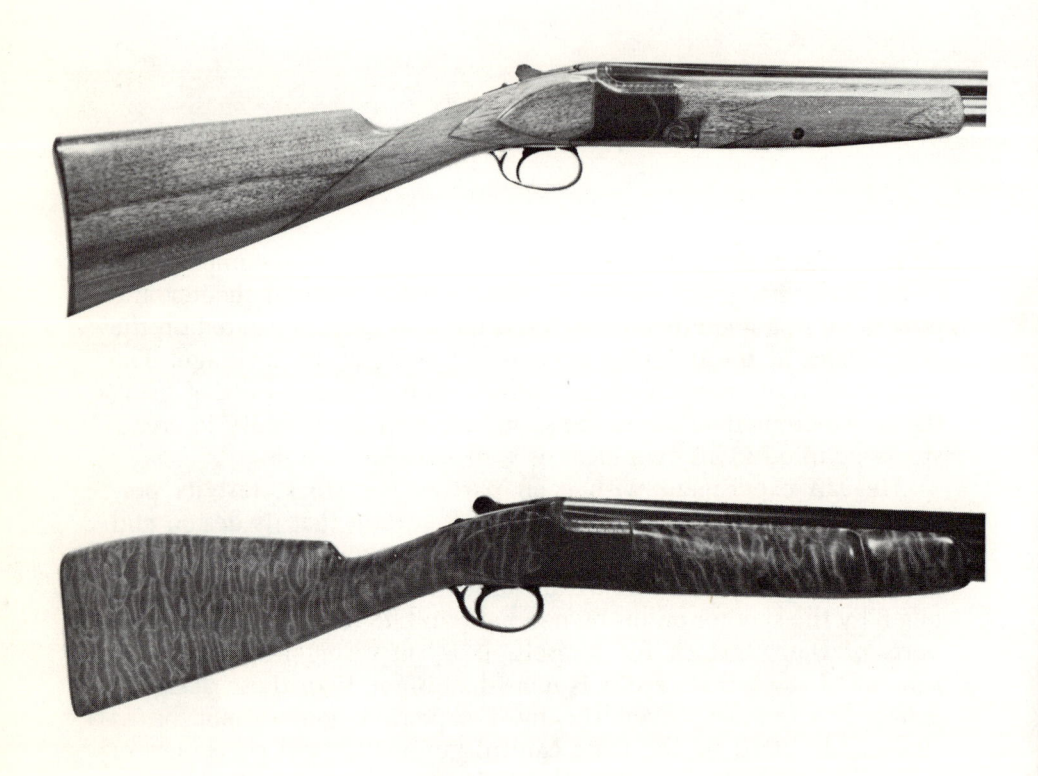

Fig. 20
Top, Conventional factory-stocked gun before rebuilding into a try-stock with Plastic Wood. (Diehl's)
Bottom, The finished try-stock was duplicated in quilted Oregon maple by a professional stock-maker, then finished by the author.

Fitting the Shotgun Stock 117

Fig. 21
Side views of this try-stock show Plastic Wood build-up of fore-end, comb, grip, and cast in finished state. The dirt of shooting and handling has been sanded off for final inspection before machine duplication.

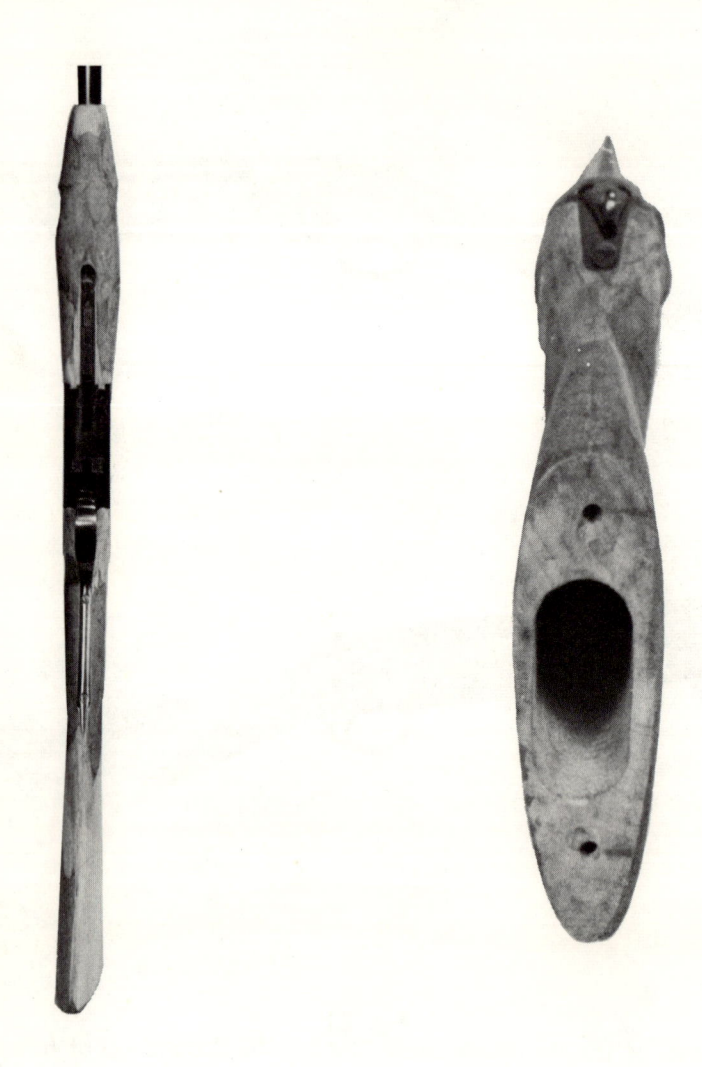

Fig. 22
Left, Underview of try-stock showing Plastic Wood buildup of submarine-shaped fore-end with experimental handhold, and tapered grip with modified Wundhammer Swell.
Right, View of butt end of try-stock showing heel in normal position (no cast) and toe cast-off by filing off wood on lower left and building up with Plastic Wood on lower right.

Experimental Shotgun Stocks 119

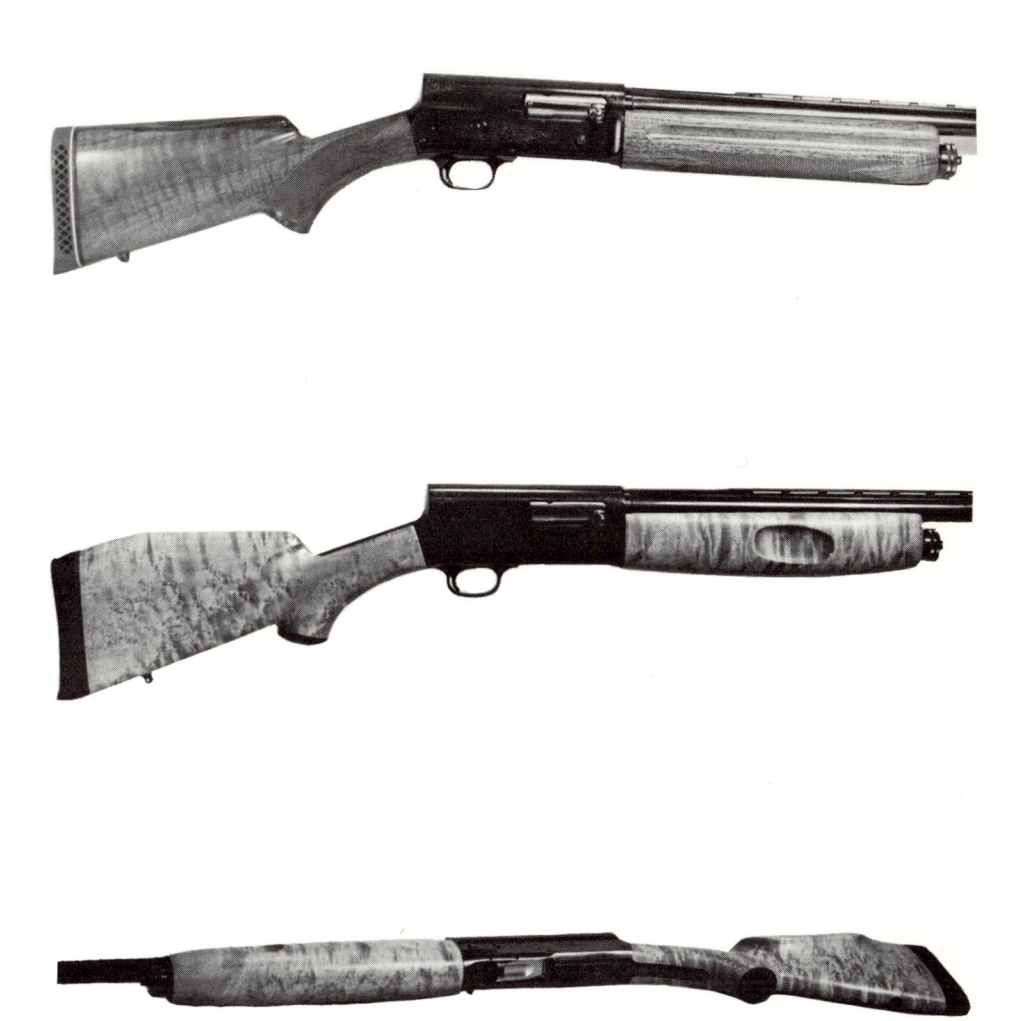

Fig. 23
Before and after pictures of this stock are disappointing to the author because the wood is of a poorer grade than expected and the grain direction of fore-arm and buttstock are not matched. The stock-making firm (not Flaig's) which duplicated the try-stock in hard maple turned the fore-arm blank 90°, so that from the side it appears to have only a curly figure, although, as shown in the lowest photograph, the birdseye figure is on the under side. Let the buyer beware.

120   The Shotgun Stock

Fig. 24
Side views of this try-stock show areas of Plastic Wood (both light and dark) and laminated balsa build-up.

Experimental Shotgun Stocks 121

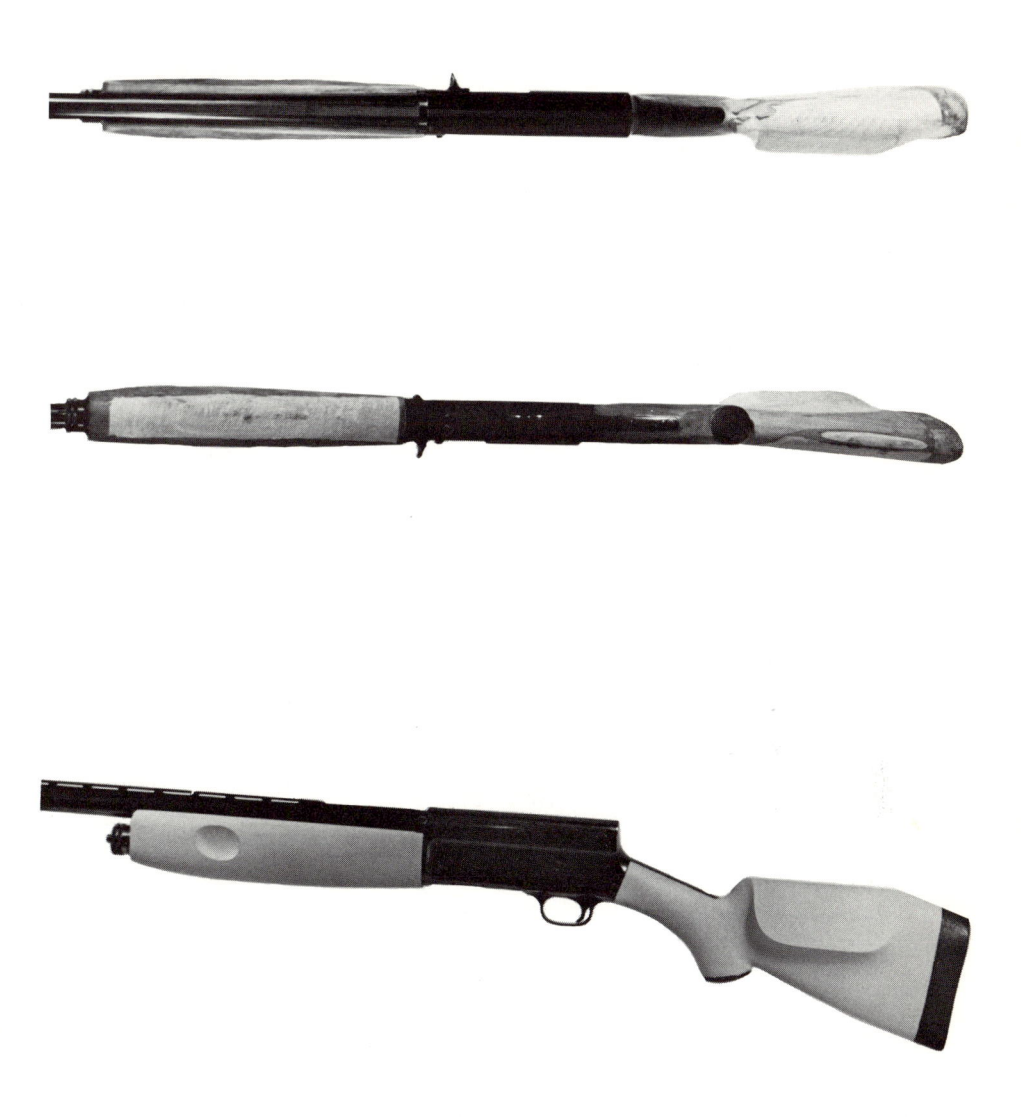

Fig. 25
The variegated appearance of a try-stock during work makes it desirable to paint it occasionally to get an overall picture of what is going on.

line-of-sight comb and cheekpiece were used, the hand-hold areas were remodeled, and an attempt was made to pull the finished design together.

The steps involved in the work are described in detail in the hope that they may help rather than bore others who make a try-stock.

OVER-AND-UNDER

The buttplate chosen was slightly wider than the one supplied commercially, less sharply tapered, and more rounded at the toe. The existing stock, which was cast-off at both heel and toe, was measured for its true center-lines after the buttplate was removed. The new buttplate was then set to the true center-line at the heel (eliminating cast-at-heel) and set to the right at the toe to increase cast-off-at-toe. Pitch and length were not changed. The edges of the buttplate were rounded after the sides of the stock had been modified to suit: the lower left edge was cut away and the lower right edge built up. Rough build-up of the comb was commenced at this time. Plastic Wood was used throughout. No attempt was made at the early stages to control the looks of the stock.

While building up the top of the comb, the forward part of the cheek-side of the body of the stock was also built out to make the comb parallel to the line of sight along the side and the top. The comb was checked from time to time by measuring down from a straightedge set in line with the top of the front sight and the top of a temporary rear sight already adjusted to produce the desired point of impact. The cheek-side of the body of the stock was measured in relation to the center line of the top of the comb to keep it parallel to the line of sight. The rear edge of the comb was sloped to the heel of the butt in a modified Greener style. The comb was brought to rough-finished completion on these measurements and the gun was tested extensively against a target board and clay pigeons. The fit was modified until it seemed as correct as possible.

During this shooting period attention was paid to the fore-arm hand position, which seemed to offer the best gun balance. This area was marked and the build-up of Plastic Wood begun there. Fore-arm grip contours were designed to fit the shape of the palm of the hand along the sides and bottom and bring the thumb and the leading edge of the second finger to rest against curved ridges or stops. When the work on the fore-arm was nearing completion, work was begun on the grip. The base-of-thumb position was first corrected by setting the notch slightly farther back and enlarging the undercut on the right. A *Wundhammer swell* type of enlargement was fash-

Experimental Shotgun Stocks

ioned on the right forward side of the grip, along with another swelling on the lower left side, both contoured to fit the hand as carefully as possible. When the grip had reached the same preliminary stage of completion as the fore-arm, the gun was again used extensively in the field and the hand-holds reworked for the best "feel" and balance.

When it was decided that the stock was satisfactory from a performance standpoint, it was reviewed from the standpoint of overall appearance. A coat of burnt-umber water color was smeared over the entire stock to suppress the lines where the light walnut met the dark Plastic Wood. The gun was then studied from a distance at different angles against a light-colored wall. The key to the general design of the side view of the stock in relation to the metal gun appeared to be in the rounded lines of the rear part of the action, which were reemphasized by the curved lines of the engraving. With these curves as a motif, the ends of the plaques at the sides of the stock between the action and the grip were changed from pointed to rounded. The underline of the stock was made slightly convex to complement the curve at the rear of the comb. The fore-arm tip was tapered to a racier curve that seemed to go with the slight belly that had been given to the underline of the fore-arm. The hand-hold areas on both the fore-arm and the grip were blended with the rest of the stock in front and behind. The sides of the body of the stock were made slightly concave lengthwise and its lower edge was tapered more sharply to save weight.

Finally, small faults in the Plastic Wood were repaired, and the contours of the stock observed carefully in a raking light to remove any undesirable hills or valleys before the try-stock was sent for copying. When the duplicated stock finally came back from the stockmaker, wood was removed from inside the buttstock and fore-arm to keep it as light as possible. Additional weight was saved by choosing a light wood (Oregon maple). No checkering was done because it was felt it would interrupt the lines of the wood figure and the over-all design of the stock and tend to prevent the shooter's hands from sliding smoothly into the proper holds on the grip and fore-arm.

SEMI-AUTOMATIC

No attempt was made to save weight in re-stocking this heavy gun. The basic procedure was the same as before, so only the differences between the two will be noted. The recoil pad was selected for its color (black), closed sides, width, and thickness (one inch). Its original basket-weave pattern was sanded smooth. The try-stock was begun by attaching a false pad of wood shaped like the new pad. A casein glue was used for this and for building up the understructure of the cheekpiece and the fore-arm with layers of $1/32$ inch sheet balsa wood. This procedure turned out to be satisfactory only where the balsa wood was subsequently covered with a fairly thick layer of Plastic Wood. The bare balsa wood was too soft to take the pressure of the tracer of the duplicating machine. For this reason, a hard veneer should be used if laminations are to be left exposed.

The false recoil pad was positioned and the sides of the body of the stock re-shaped before the cheekpiece and comb were built up, so that no change would need be made later in the contour of the side of the stock around the cheekpiece. The alignment of the comb was carried out on the same principle as before, keeping the flat of the cheekpiece in parallel with the line of sight in both planes. Control of cheek pressure was found to be more difficult than anticipated. The first version had to be changed after shooting trials at a target board showed that too much pressure had been applied to the cheek while testing fit with the temporary sight. The depth of the cheekpiece was set slightly below the shooter's jaw line. The rear of the cheekpiece was blended to the side of the stock by a gentle S-curve to avoid sharp face-banging rear edges. The concavity below the front edge of the cheekpiece was needed to blend the line-of-sight design with the grip because it is thicker toward the front than the usual taper-sided cheekpiece. This also seemed to give a pleasing contour to a cheekpiece that is somewhat bulkier than many.

The grip could not be modified as much as was desired because of the straight upper tang and the only slightly curved lower tang of this particular gun. However, the under surface of the grip beyond the tang was curved slightly forward and the angle of its cap changed to shorten it. The grip was slightly thickened toward the muzzle. A black pistol-grip cap was added to match the black recoil pad. The fore-end was widened and deepened and tapered to be thicker toward the muzzle. Slots were cut well below the shooter's line of vision to exactly fit the thumb on the left and the last three fingers on the right. This specific positioning is only practical in a gun not intended for speed-mounting, but works out very well for shooting where there is a little more time.

These oval slots gave an interesting look to the fore-arm and seemed to relate to the curves at the ends of the cheekpiece. The same procedure of study of the gun's overall design was followed as before, without any great result except to modify the curves of the underlines of the fore-arm and buttstock to make them seem to repeat the curve of the comb. The cheekpiece and the slots in the

Experimental Shotgun Stocks

fore-arm seemed to contribute naturally to the gun's appearance without any decorative intention having entered into their development.

Both stocks have proved very satisfactory in the field. Working with the try-stock method offers the shooter a chance to experiment with, test, and learn about the shotgun stock in a way that is only slightly less enjoyable than bringing home the elusive grouse.

V
THE WOOD

19
Gunstock Woods

The shooter can only choose from among a relatively small number of guns each exactly like its own kind. In the choice of wood for his gunstock, as in its design and fit, the shooter has an opportunity to make his shotgun his own.

Perhaps more than any other object fabricated from it, the gunstock makes full use of the nature of wood, exploiting both its physical properties and its figure. The suitability of any wood for gunstocks depends first of all on its physical properties. The generally accepted physical criteria are summarized in Table No. 6,

TABLE NO. 6. THE PHYSICAL PROPERTIES OF GUNSTOCK WOODS.

General Terms	Scientific Terms
Suitable weight.	Specific gravity. Weight (lbs. per ft.^{3}, 12% moisture).
Hardness, dent resistance.	Load to embed ball to ½ diam. in side or end.
Minimal swelling or shrinkage on wetting or drying.	Volume shrinkage, % (green to 6% moisture).
Works easily.	Machining characteristics, (rating).
Toughness, strength, elasticity, shock-resistance, not brittle, will not split.	Shear strength, (P.S.I.). Static bending, (load). Impact bending, (weight-distance).

which correlates older descriptive phrases with the scientific terms used in wood testing. Unsuited for scientific measurement, but very

129

important to the stockmaker, is the traditional specification of uniformity of density and texture. Table No. 7 compares the tested

TABLE NO. 7. THE PHYSICAL PROPERTIES OF SOME AMERICAN GUNSTOCK WOODS COMPARED.

Name of Wood	Weight at 12% moisture. lbs./ft.^{3}	Impact bending. Height of drop causing complete failure. 50 lb. hammer. Inches.	Hardness. To embed 0.444 in. ball to ½ diameter. Side, lbs.
ASH	34–41	33–40	1210
BEECH	45	41	1300
BIRCH	38–44	52	1340
CHERRY	35	29	950
SUGAR MAPLE	44	39	1450
OREGON MAPLE	34	28	850
SYCAMORE	34	26	770
BLACK WALNUT	38	34	1010

physical properties of some American gunstock woods.[80] Walnut's balanced combination of these measurable characteristics (Table No. 7) can be accepted as the norm for gunstock woods.

Weight is particularly important in shotgun stock woods. The generally acceptable weight range is between 35 and 40 pounds per cubic foot at 12 percent moisture content. Lighter woods are generally progressively deficient in hardness and may be deficient in toughness. Some otherwise desirable woods are too heavy, except where total gun weight is not a consideration. Wood test figures themselves, however, are statistical averages compiled from tests of many samples of a given type wood. Dr. Wayne Murphy emphasizes that, among different samples of a particular wood, variations as great as + or —50% may occur in physical properties.[81] Ergo, the importance of evaluating the physical properties of each stock blank on its own merits rather than by label. This concept is independent of the variations in properties within a single stock blank, soft spots or splits (Fig. 27, Left). Proper drying is vital to the physical soundness of any stock blank. While the drying technique itself must be correctly employed, neither general method of drying, air or kiln, has any essential superiority for producing a successful result.

Claims are sometimes made that walnut is superior and maple faulty in resistance to deterioration attributed to contact with gun

Gunstock Woods

oil. Wood deterioration, generally seen when the buttstock is removed and the inletted area examined, does happen in walnut and other woods as well as in maple. Dr. Murphy attributes this condition entirely to wood damage by moisture at a location where water can enter but satisfactory drying may not occur.[81] As evidence he cites the fact that such deterioration is not seen in the oil-treated "gun-blocks" of hard maple used in naval ordnance.

The stocks of better shotguns are all two-piece affairs. Quality for quality, superior wood is available at a given price in the shorter blanks required for shotguns. Warping, which is a problem with long one-piece rifle stocks, is not a factor in shotgun stocks as regards accuracy. When it comes to layout and inletting, however, the shotgun stock makes considerable demands on wood quality and structure.

The stock is weakest where it is attached to the gun, and where the grip is narrowest. Its grain must run so that there is a sound structural continuity between the metal gun and the body of the stock. The direction of the grain must be in line with the direction of the force of recoil (Fig. 26). While layout is relatively easy with straight-grained wood, irregular figures present a problem (Fig. 27, Left). Decorative figures that reduce the strength of the wood must be largely confined to the body of the stock, so that the grain is straight in the grip. The stocks of two-barreled guns are fragile at the juncture of wood and metal in proportion to the amount of excavation needed to inlet the tangs and the mechanism between them. Some actions have been notorious in this respect. The use of bedding substances may reduce the risk of the stock splitting because of inexact fit at the point of attachment.

Deep U-shaped inletting is required for the fore-arms of repeating and over-and-under guns. The wood is wrapped around barrels and magazines as a thin shell that can easily split even though it is straight-grained. Most straight-sided commercial fore-arms are weaker toward the rear. Some makers strengthen this area by inserting a supporting band of tough wood whose grain runs at a right angle to that of the wood of the fore-arm. However, even the best reinforcement may not suffice unless the fore-arm design itself is strong. Central thickening will make the fore-arm more rigid, like a submarine.

When the buttstock is to be hollowed extensively, highly figured woods of inherently fragile structure should be avoided. With such woods, weight can best be saved by slimming the outside of the body of the stock forward of the buttplate, using only a small internal cavity or none. Similarly, such figured wood should only be used for thicker fore-arm designs.

The use of laminated wood for shotgun stocks can eliminate

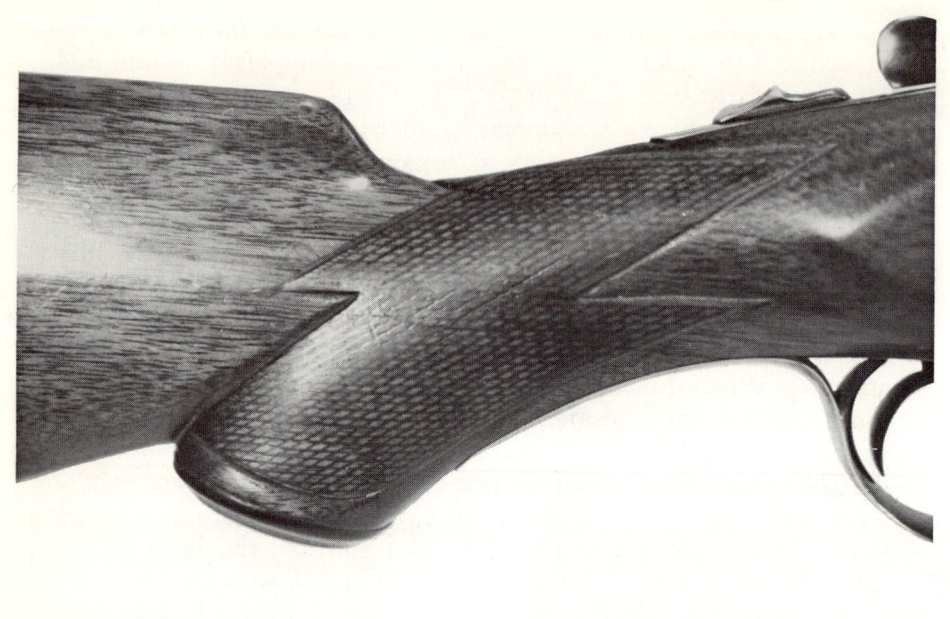

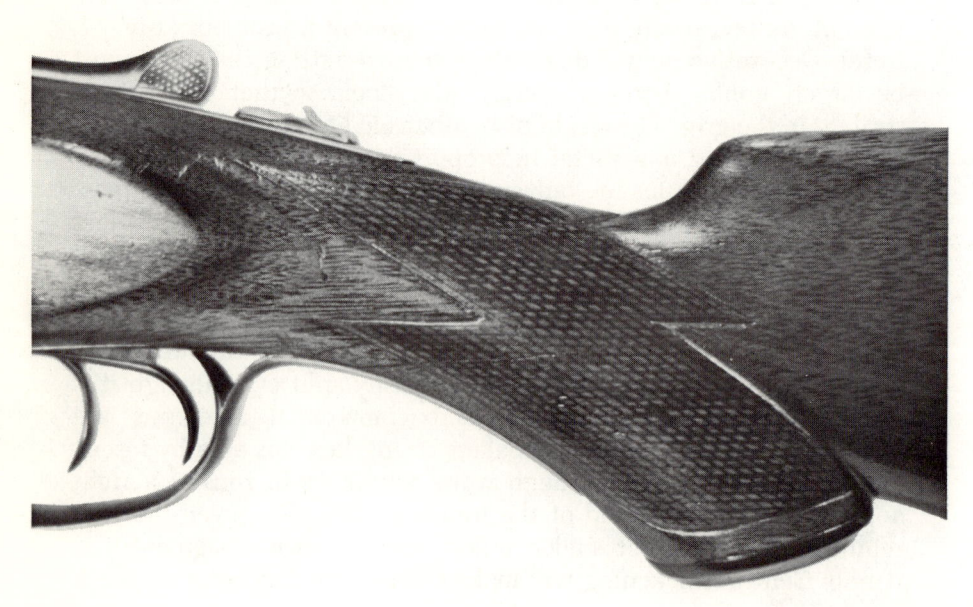

Fig. 26
Poor stock layout on an otherwise sound piece of walnut caused this (repaired) stock to crack in several places at the grip because the grain runs diagonally instead of lengthwise to the stress the wood must withstand. The cracks reopened after a few hundred rounds.

Gunstock Woods   133

Fig. 27
Left, Some attractively figured wood may have too numerous or serious imperfections or a grain structure that is architecturally unsound for use as a gunstock. This blank has many splits and an impossible grain.
Right, This blank has a very fine stump figure covering about two thirds of its area. It is shown because it is typical of the great majority of figured blanks available, whose figures are not complete throughout the wood. Compare this blank with the rare perfectly distributed stump pattern in Fig. 17.

structural problems inherent in natural wood. Its lack of popularity with shotgunners is probably based on aesthetic considerations. With the exception of a few specialized camping and anti-recoil stocks, plastics have probably failed to catch on for the same reason. Moreover, plastics do not lend themselves to fitting or remodeling, and their easily scratched surfaces cannot be refinished (Fig. 35, Bottom).

When the physical properties of woods used for shotgun stocks are reasonably equal, a distinction can be made between those whose grain structure is only architecturally suitable for gunstocks and those that are also decorative. Some woods that make excellent gunstocks are simply not good looking. Other woods that make equally practical stocks can have very beautiful figures. Among the woods that can have really good decorative figures, superb blanks completely figured on both sides (Fig. 28) are rarer than blanks whose figures are incomplete (Figs. 27, Right; 29). Undistinguished blanks are common in even the best decorative woods.

There is probably more to be said for a deliberately unpretentious stock than for one made of a highly reputed wood whose figure does not correspond to its price. The shooting public has been oversold on the name of the wood. While better factory guns are almost never sold with structurally unsound stocks, they are just as rarely sold with really good wood figures at whatever price. The shooter should be prepared to judge a blank or a stock for its intrinsic merits. It is easily possible to pay a high price for not much. The shooter who really looks at the individual piece of wood can find bargains in plain practical woods and can buy fine decorative pieces of some woods for less money than others.

The elements that comprise what is admired as figure are the grain of the wood and its color.[82] The appearance called grain is caused by the textural differences peculiar to the cellular arrangement of growing trees that can be seen on the ends of a log or stump: the annual rings and the medullary rays.

The concentric annual rings, representing each year's growth of new wood, are composed of the relatively porous early or spring wood and the less porous late or summer wood. Gunstock woods like American walnut are classified as ring-porous because their spring wood is rather coarse and porous in comparison with that of diffuse-porous even-grained woods like maple whose pores are nearly uniformly small and whose annual rings are less conspicuous (Fig. 30). The other basic grain structure, the medullary rays, can be seen as narrow bands of wood cells radiating out from the center of the stump.

The art of sawing and laying out blanks, which can bring out

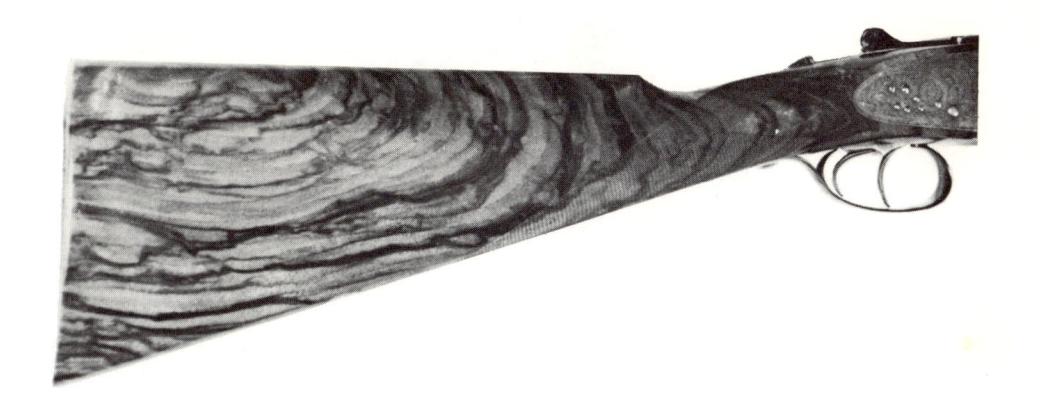

Gunstock Woods   135

Fig. 28
This English "best" gun stocked with pigment-figure **Juglans regia** superbly marked on both sides and throughout its length exemplifies the perfection attainable by decorative wood of the very highest quality. (Abercrombie and Fitch)

SAPWOOD   ANNUAL RINGS

HEARTWOOD   MEDULLARY RAYS

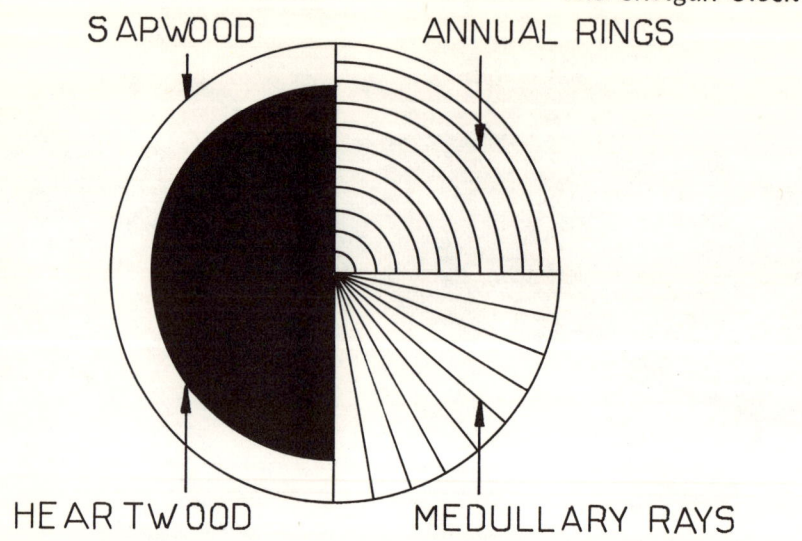

or botch whatever figure the wood has to offer, can be understood by thinking in terms of cross, radial, and tangential sections of the log.

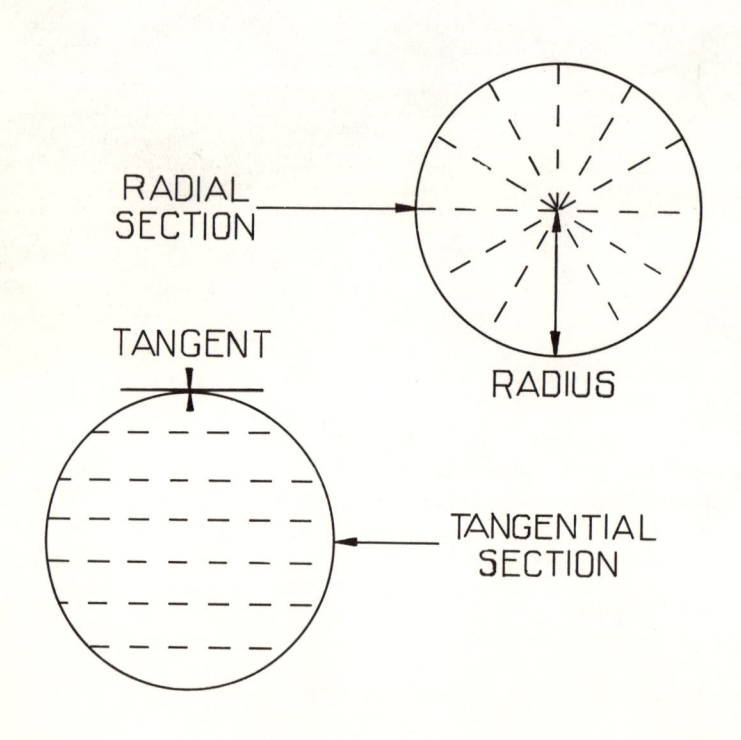

RADIAL SECTION

RADIUS

TANGENT

TANGENTIAL SECTION

Gunstock Woods   137

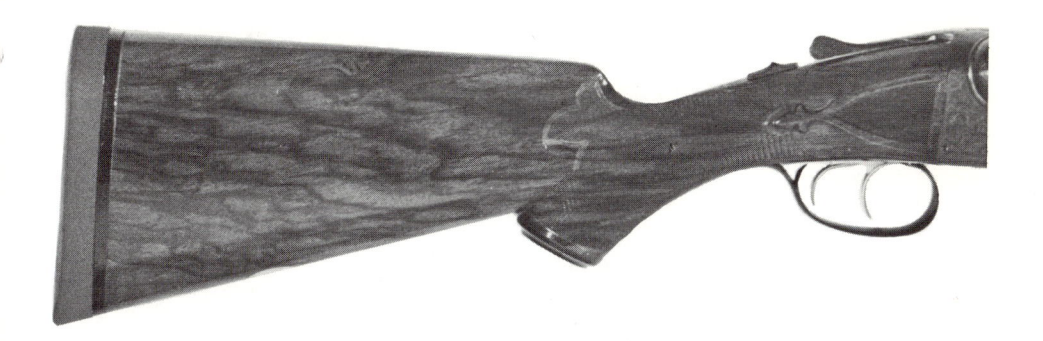

Fig. 29
While the pigment-figure walnut of this stock has very considerable merit, it is illustrated because it is less than perfect. It is one-sided, the figure being nearly complete on the right, but incomplete at comb and toe on the left. Unfortunately, the quality of figure offered today on many very high priced guns is often much poorer than that on this modest Parker. (Coll. Dr. Robert C. Snavely)

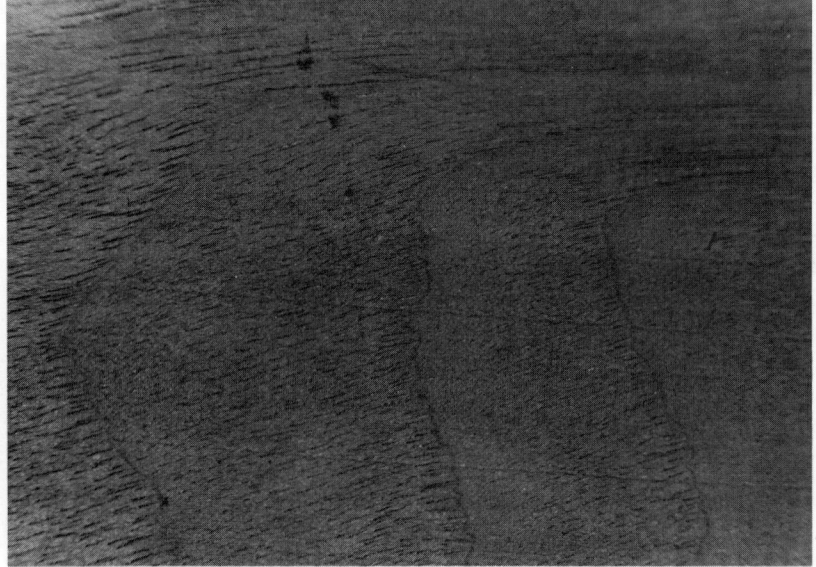

Fig. 30
Top, Magnified view of unsanded hard maple showing its uniformly fine diffuse-porous grain with very little distinction between spring wood and summer wood. The irregular wave structure of the grain can be clearly seen in relation to the curly figure it causes. (Flaig's)
Bottom, This magnified view of diagonally cut unsanded American black walnut clearly shows the changes that mark the annual growth cycle from spring wood (coarse texture) to summer wood (fine texture) of this ring-porous tree. The need for filling the grain is apparent. (Flaig's)

Gunstock Woods

Most gunstock blanks must be made from straight-grained wood. Their figure depends on how the angle of the saw-cut and the position of the blank relative to the center of the log affect the annual rings. As the location of the blank changes from close to the center of the log to nearer its outer surface, the diameter of the annual rings increases so that they curve less as they pass through the blank. As the blank's angle of approach to the center of the log varies, the annual rings arc through it in different directions. Plain- (flat- or slab-sawed) gunstock blanks are cut so that the flat side of the blank is more or less a tangential section of the log, the annual rings appearing on the side of the stock as a contour-line or *leaf* figure (Fig. 31). Quarter-sawed blanks are cut so that the flat side of the blank is a near radial section of the log, and the annual rings appear on the side of the stock as nearly parallel lines (Fig. 32). In woods with prominent medullary rays, quarter-sawing may expose the rays at right angles to the annual rings, because the direction of the quarter-cut is parallel to the direction of the rays. Such figures, called *ray-fleck* or *silver grain*, are familiar in sycamore cut in this manner.

Variations in the pattern of growth of the wood grain elements produce more complicated figures. In some trees spiral clockwise growth of the cells of the annual rings alternates at intervals of several years with counter-clockwise growth. This type of reversing spiral in the annual rings produces what is called interlocked-grain wood. When such wood is quarter-sawed the alternating longitudinal figure due to the change in grain direction is called *ribbon* or *stripe* figure. If the lengthwise stripes are at least a foot in length the figure is termed *broken stripe*, if shorter, *roe*.

Tree cell growth in wave form in either the radial or tangential plane causes some of the most remarkable wood figures. Waves of various sizes which give the wood a corrugated appearance when split radially produce *fiddleback* (Fig. 33) and *curly* (Fig. 30) figures. Pocket-shaped wave structures in the annular rings produce distinctive figures in maple according to their size and shapes when the wood is cut tangentially. The small navel-shaped *birdseye* of hard maple is thought to be due to a tendency to form dormant buds (Fig. 35, Top). The larger bubble-shaped *blister*, and the still larger more irregularly convex *quilted* figures occur in Oregon maple (Fig. 20 Bottom; 9, Bottom).

Undulating cell growth produces twisted grain patterns classified as *crotch, stump,* or *burl* figures. *Feather* or *swirl* crotch figures which occur where branching takes place, (Fig. 34) and stump figures from the bell-shaped base of the tree make some of the most handsomely symmetrical twisted-grain gunstocks (Fig. 17; 27,

140   The Shotgun Stock

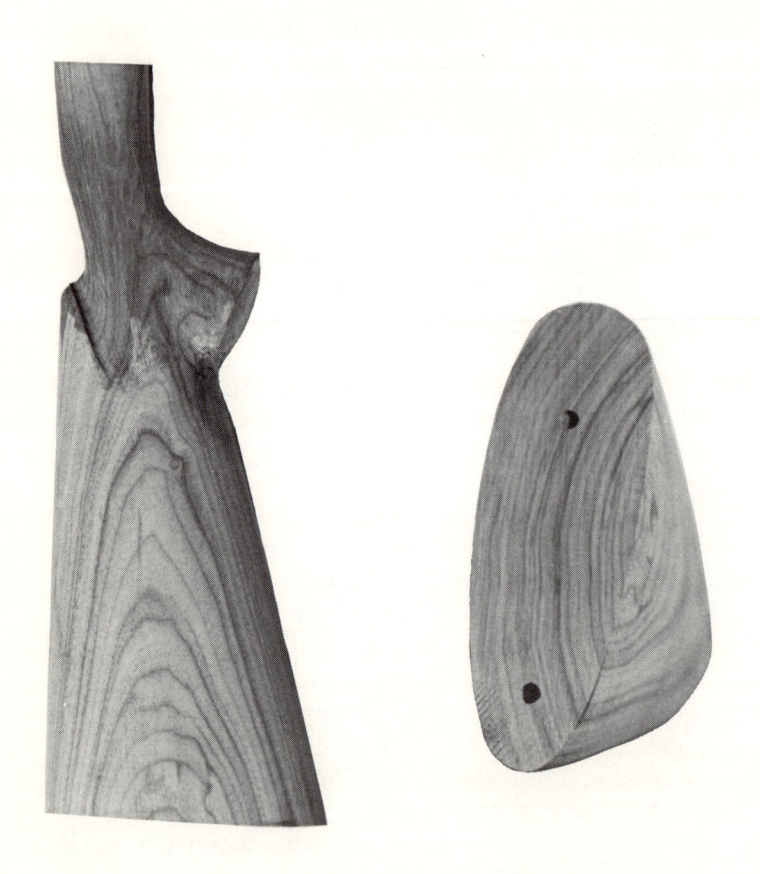

Fig. 31
This unfinished walnut buttstock photographed from the side to show a typical figure produced by slab- (flat-, plain-,) sawing. The slightly diagonal photograph of the butt indicates the relation of slab-sawing to the stump. (Flaig's)

Gunstock Woods 141

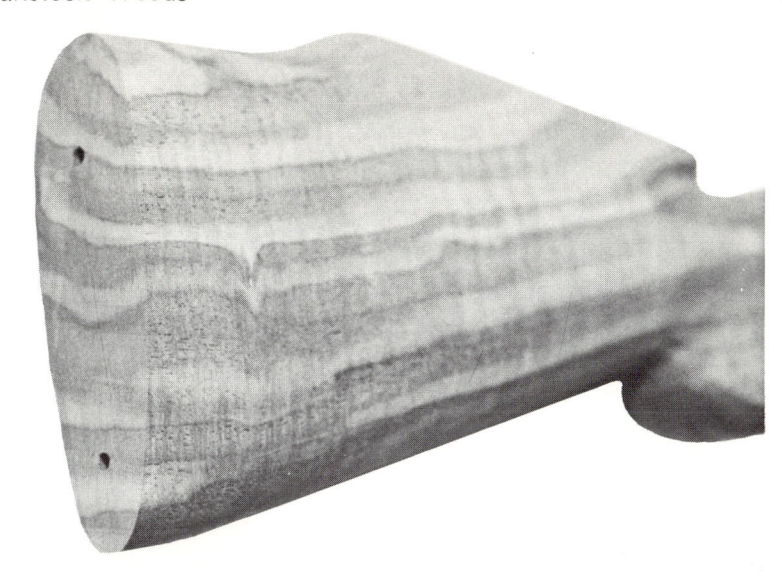

Fig. 32
Top, Claro walnut; **bottom,** Circassian walnut. Photographs of unfinished buttstocks showing typical grain patterns produced by quartersawing. The direction of the grain through the butt shows how the blank was cut in relation to the stump. Each has a pigment-type stripe figure typical of its wood. (Flaig's)

Fig. 33
Left, A fiddleback figure is uniformly distributed throughout this quarter-sawn walnut buttstock blank, at right-angles to its longitudinal stripe. (Flaig's)
Right, The wave form of the grain of the unsanded walnut seen in this magnified close-up is the structural basis for fiddleback figures. (Flaig's)

Gunstock Woods 143

Fig. 34
The crotch figure on both sides of this very exceptional Claro walnut blank is of uniformly high quality. The blank itself has been correctly cut so that the stockmaker can make the most of it when he lays out his pattern. (Flaig's)

Right). The wood from burls (burrs), large tumor-like abnormalities formed on the tree in response to injury or fire, has completely irregular twisted figures. Fine examples of any type of twisted grain figure can have as spectacular a decorative effect as wood offers. However, these figures often contain structural weaknesses. While the photographs have been chosen to illustrate typical figures, combination and transitional figures are frequently found.

The second basic element of wood figure is color. The color seen in the wood is due to extraneous pigmentary substances that infiltrate it during the tree's life history and become concentrated in different proportions within its framework. In its most familiar form the inactive older inner wood darkens and is called heartwood, while the newer light-colored outer wood is called sapwood. Sapwood is not generally used for gunstocks because of its pallor. The term *stripe,* previously used in regard to interlocked grain, is also used for linear figures that result from color variations in the annual rings instead of from changes due to alternate spiraling (Fig. 32). The term *pigment figure* is used to designate figures due to the irregular penetration of coloring materials related to or independent of the grain structure. It may take bizarre forms: "marbling" in some grades of walnut (Fig. 28), parallel stripes of alternate colors as in the case of zebra wood, or abrupt random changes in wood color sometimes called "crazy", although the latter term may be used to describe any wood of completely irregular figure. Marked color tone changes of large areas within a blank may also be due to wood grafting.

Information about the availability of woods can be obtained from catalogs of the larger stockmaking firms, or by personal contact with them or with independent dealers, stockmakers, and gunsmiths, or even local cutters. If at all possible, arrangements should be made to see the individual piece of wood before purchase. Some dealers will send wood on approval. Finished gunstocks of exceptional wood can be seen at exhibitions of antique firearms, the annual meeting of the National Rifle Association, and in first-rate arms collections such as that of the Winchester Museum at New Haven, Connecticut, or the Metropolitan Museum in New York. British gunstocks of the highest quality can be seen at Abercrombie and Fitch in New York. Perhaps the best place to visualize the full potential of beautifully figured wood is in great collections of antique furniture and musical instruments, such as those at the Metropolitan, where the gun zealot is not distracted by the sight of firearms.

Inexpensive stock woods offered by the gunstock trade or obtainable locally in the United States, include:

apple beech birch cherry pecan sycamore	Satisfactory for weight and properties but usually have no outstanding color or figure.
ash persimmon	Usually undistinguished in appearance. Occasional pieces may have fine decorative qualities and may be expensive.
maple mahogany myrtle walnut	Relatively inexpensive in plain grades.

Good practical stocks can be made of beech (45 lbs.), ash (34-41 lbs.), and apple (48 lbs.) wood, obtained locally. Beech and apple are heavy. Beech and ash are light-colored; apple is brown. No decorative figure can be expected except in the unusual "curly ash." Stockmakers offer inexpensive grades of cherry (35 lbs.), birch (38-44 lbs.), mahogany (25-53 lbs.), pecan (39-49 lbs.), persimmon (49 lbs.), and sycamore (34 lbs.). Cherry may be the most satisfactory of these woods. Its surface is dense, its leathery color is warm, and its properties are generally desirable. Occasional quarter or slab-cut blanks may have very pleasing figures. Pecan and ordinary persimmon are brown, birch is white to pale yellow, sycamore greenish-yellow to brown. The lacy figure in sycamore ("lace-wood") looks better in radially cut boards than in the shaped stock. All meet minimum stocking standards. Woods other than walnut are now frequently used to stock less expensive guns. Walnut and other decorative woods command higher prices for quality than formerly. While often attributed to the scarcity of the traditional woods, price competition actually preempts the better grades for veneer rather than gunstocks.

Woods advertised by American commercial sources as stocks or blanks for shotguns at the time of writing are:

birch	pecan
cherry	persimmon
lacewood	rosewood
laminated woods	sycamore
madrone	vermilion
maple (hard, Oregon)	walnut (American, Circassian, Claro, French, hybrid)
mesquite (flatpod, screw-pod)	
myrtle	zebra
padouk	

Readers interested in other exotic woods should consult Alexander L. Howard's fascinating *A Manual of The Timbers of the World*.[83] Commercially available woods that can offer fine decorative figures are described below in detail.

CURLY ASH; Hungarian ash (33-40 lbs.): Some species of North American ash occasionally produce wood with a very fine regular curl figure designated as curly ash. White to light brown color, it is worth looking for locally.

LACEWOOD; silky oak; *Grevillea robusta* (33-37 lbs.): Quarter-sawn blanks of this light brown Australian wood exhibit a very fine ray-fleck figure called *clash*. The wood offered by one American stockmaker is in the extreme light-weight range.

LAMINATED WOODS: These are principally used when extreme stability is desired in rifle stocks. The wood layers are fastened together with moisture-resistant glues, in thicknesses from $\frac{1}{28}$ to $\frac{5}{16}$ inch. When alternate layers of contrasting woods are used the finished stock has a flashy contour-map figure. Woods offered commercially are: walnut-walnut, maple-maple, maple-walnut, maple-cherry, walnut-birch, walnut-madrone, and madrone-birch. Their high degree of stability has nothing to contribute to shotgun accuracy. The shooter who chooses this wood must do so for its striking appearance. Properly made up it will be as permanent as the woods used, or more so.

MADRONE; Pacific madrone; madroña; *Arbutus menziesi* (43 lbs.): This hard light reddish-brown wood, native to the North American west coast, is claimed by some stockmakers to possess all the fine qualities of walnut except figure. Processing problems with excessive shrinking during drying are said to have been solved.

MAHOGANY (25-53 lbs.): In its best figured grades, it can rival any other wood in decorative quality, but has been accused of brittleness. Provided the particular piece of mahogany has desirable weight and properties it should make an interesting gunstock. Suitable varieties include: Honduran mahogany, *Swietenia macrophylla*, and African mahogany, *Khaya grandifolia*. Philippine mahoganies, *Shorea eximia, S. nigrosensis,* generally lack the necessary physical characteristics.

MAPLE (34-44 lbs.): The many North American genera are classified as yielding hard or soft timber. The very dense, pale to reddish-brown, heavy, "hard, white rock maple" comes from the sugar maple, *Acer saccharum* and black maple, *Acer nigrum*. Hard maple offers remarkable wave figures, curly, fiddleback, and one-of-a-kind birds-eye and near birds-eye (*Patapsco,* or *Papapsco* wood) figures. Its physical properties more than meet stockmaking requirements. Soft maple from the red maple, *Acer rubrum,* and the silver maple,

Gunstock Woods

Acer saccharinum, is light brown to grayish, greenish or purplish, and lighter in weight. Its gunstock properties are at the borderline or inadequate. Oregon maple, big leaf maple, *Acer macrophyllum,* while sometimes called soft maple, is classified separately by the authors of the *Textbook of Wood Technology* because its physical properties are intermediate between those of hard and true soft maple. This pinkish-brown wood meets performance standards for light-weight gunstock woods, and offers the unique blister and quilted figures. Oregon maple may have the lightest weight for properties of any readily available stock wood of comparable quality.

Maple has fallen from its former state of grace with the shooting public, perhaps because light-colored woods are generally out of fashion (Fig. 35, Top). It can be selected for color, stained, or preferably darkened by flaming to have deeper tones ranging from pinkish gold to dark golden brown and orange brown. All maple enthusiasts should read Hartley's account of the selection of maple and the "Siugi" flaming process.[84] Maple once gave a distinctively national character to American gunstocks. Perhaps it could do so again if stockmakers would emphasize the possibilities of its warmer, darker colors.

MESQUITE: Native to the arid parts of the west coast of the Americas, this scrubby tree has a large tap root, but small trunk diameter. Of two varieties used for gunstocks, screw-pod mesquite, screw-bean mesquite, *Strombocarpa odorata, Prosopis pubescens,* yields a brown to reddish colored flamboyantly figured coarse-grained wood resembling oak. It seems to be valued for its appearance and "western" connotations rather than for any particularly suitable properties. The wood often has defects due to the small size and irregular shape of the trunk. Flat-pod mesquite, *Prosopis glandulosa,* is claimed to have properties better suited for gunstocks, particularly stability. Its grain is denser, with figure similar to run-of-the-mill walnut.

MYRTLE; Oregon myrtle; California laurel; *Umbellularia californica:* This moderately hard medium-weight wood comes from the North American Pacific coast. In contrast to the regular patterns obtainable in walnut or maple, this native wood may produce figures of such startling irregularity that it is said no two blanks are alike (Fig. 36). Colors also vary widely, ranging from a light rich brown or grayish-brown to yellows, greenish tones, and near-blacks. Figures range from fairly even stripes and curls, to birds-eyes, to strangely mixed swirling and twisting figures suiting the most rakish temperament. It forms, with walnut and maple, the big three of American stock woods. There is some confusion about the source

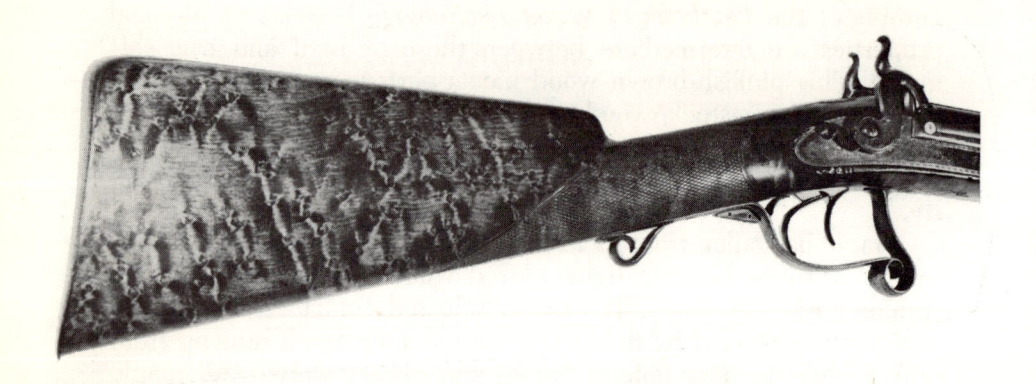

Fig. 35
Top, This Purdey stocked in fine curly birdseye should remind Americans that over a hundred years ago even English "best" shotgun makers thought highly of our native maple whose figure gains in intensity and depth with age. (Abercrombie and Fitch)
Bottom, The scratches accumulated during the brief life of this plastic stock are unrepairable. Of course it isn't the fault of the plastic that this may also be the all time champion ugly stock design.

Fig. 36

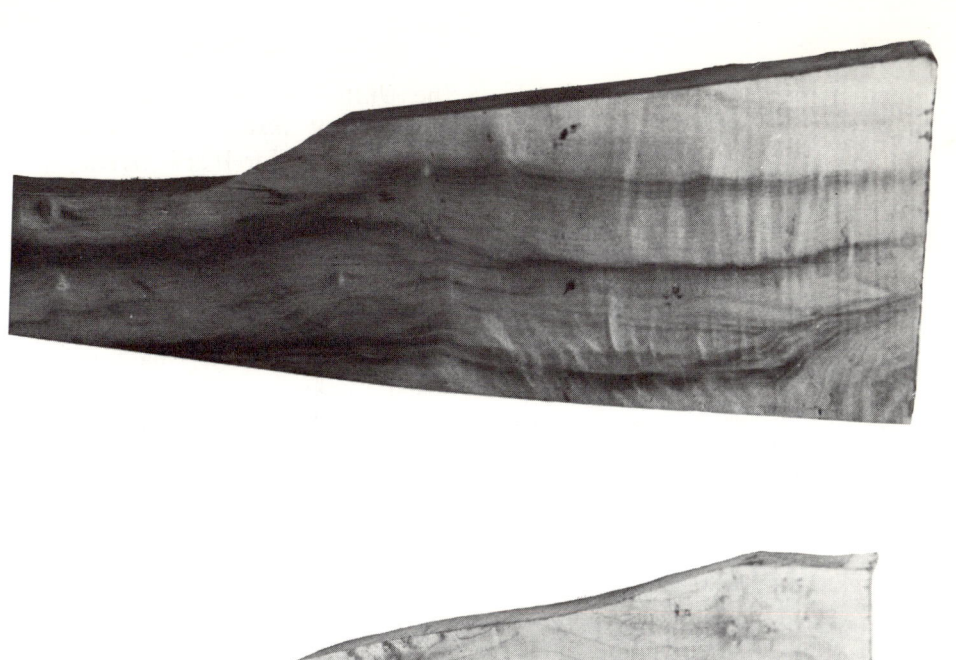

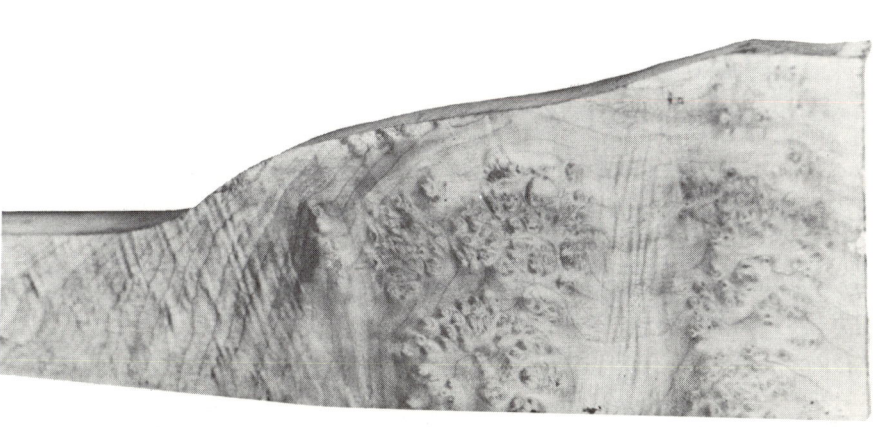

Oregon Myrtle: No other American wood offers such a variety of unusual, irregularly colored and patterned figures that are both beautiful and structurally sound for gunstocks. This wood varies widely in weight; either light or heavy blanks can be found. (Flaig's)

and nomenclature of wood sold in the United States as "myrtle". Howe stated that blackbean, *Castanospermum australe*, was sold under that name here.[85] Baker claimed the same for black myrtle, *Cargillia pentamera*. Both are Australian and somewhat heavier than walnut.[86] The variety of colors and figure they offer may explain some of the wide variation seen in "myrtle".

PADOUK; golden padouk; *Pterocarpus dalbergoides;* Andaman padouk; *P. macrocarpus;* Burma padouk (48-61 lbs.): This heavy oriental wood, recommended by one dealer for stocking magnum rifles, can be used for heavier shotguns. Its color is reddish-brown. The best figure is described as stripe or roe, which may be broken or mottled. *Vermilion* is a bright red or crimson variety of this wood. The color is said to fade on exposure to sunlight and heat after cutting, but to be color-fast after finishing. Its physical properies are suitable for gunstocks.

PERSIMMON; *Diospyros virginiana* (49 lbs.): Anyone who sees this native wood in old tools will be impressed with its hardness and polishability. Exceptional figured pieces characterized by light yellow to brown or near-black streaks are worth trying to locate. The heartwood which provides this desirable pigment figure is unusually small.

ROSEWOOD; Brazilian rosewood; *Dalbergia nigra* (47-56 lbs.): This heavy wood is suitable for the stocking of shotguns where weight is not a factor in wood selection. It is cut from several different species of trees having similar wood: yellow to chocolate brown with dark brown to black streaking, the darks sometimes have a purplish cast. Pao rosa, *Physocalymma floridum* (50-60 lbs.), called "rose-wood" inside Brazil, is yellowish to rose-colored.

VERMILION: See Padouk.

WALNUT (38 lbs.): The physical properties of this wood make it the standard gunstock material. When they are combined with the color and figure of which its best pieces are capable, results can be close to perfection. Different species (about 17, plus hybrids) offer wood of different characteristics, as can the same species when grown under different conditions in different places. It is so widely available under different names in different grades that it is more important to judge each piece of it on its own merits than any other stock wood. The classic walnut is *Juglans regia* (Persian, English, Spanish, French, Italian, Turkish, Circassian). The characteristics of this wood vary by country of origin and by locale within that country. National designations, regardless of origin, are also used as trade descriptive terms. When the wood is of light color and weight, with fairly dense grain, it may be designated "French walnut". "English walnut" is sometimes used ambiguously to describe fine imported

Gunstock Woods

Juglans regia when used to stock English "best" guns. Stripe or swirl pigment-figure walnut may be called "Circassian". The best *Juglans regia* is characterized by its density and uniformity, as much as by its figure. Indifferent figure is also produced everywhere.

American black walnut, eastern black walnut, *Juglans nigra*, is always coarser grained than *J. regia* varieties, and of a more uniformly brown color. It is capable of beautiful dark tones of near-black, gold, purplish and orange. It generally has less color contrast than the best *J. regia* and pigment figures of the highest quality are rare. The wood color improves with age and antique wood should be looked for locally. Fiddleback, broken stripe, crotch, and stump figures characterize its best moments rather than the pigment figures of *J. regia*. Its plain wood can be very plain.

Of other indigenous walnuts: Arizona black walnut, *J. major;* California black walnut, *J. californica;* Northern California black walnut, *J. hindsi;* and Texas black walnut, *J. rupestri* have been used for gunstocks. *Hindsi* and *rupestri* are said to offer better figured woods. "Claro walnut" is sometimes used as a trade term for the wood of *J. hindsi*, but it is also used to describe crosses of *J. californica* and *J. hindsi* with *J. nigra* and other species. Individual Claro blanks may be outstanding, with dramatic color contrast (Fig. 32 Top, Fig. 34). Japanese walnut, *J. sieboldiana cordiformis* is also used for gunstocks. East Indian walnut, *Albizzia lebbek* (47-65 lbs.) is not a walnut but has properties and figure suitable for heavy stocks. African walnut, tigerwood, *Lovea klaineana* (31 lbs.) seems to be the prize exotic, for it combines the virtuous physical properties of walnut (which it is not) with extraordinary figures and light weight. It is said to have good stripe or roe figures, but is most remarkable for curved and twisting figures called blister or *snail*. Its color is golden to dark brown. It comes from Benin and Lagos (Nigeria).

ZEBRA WOOD: is offered by one stockmaker who claims only "fair" stability for it at a weight of 42-46 lbs. In commercial practice at least three variegated woods of bright color have been given this name.

20
Gunstock Finishes

There is a persistent air of mystery about the subject of wood finishing. That "lost" materials and techniques used by old violin and furniture makers, or London oil finishes and French polishes used by traditional gun-makers, should be regarded as unattainably perfect is irrational today. We live in a period of unparalleled development of the technology of surface coatings. New and often better materials and faster and simpler processes are continually appearing. Mystery also survives in the form of manufacturers' exasperating, if not nefarious, policies of secrecy in regard to the ingredients and properties of their products. The mere number of trade-names advertised for use in stock finishing, let alone for general wood finishing, is confusing. No stockmaker can compare the relative merits of new preparations with those of old materials and methods unless he has worked with them and had the opportunity to examine the results on stocks that have been used over a period of time.

How is the simple shotgunner to find his way through this maze? His problem is to evaluate gunstock finishes, whether he actually intends to do the finishing himself, or orders a certain finish, or buys a finished stock. This section will try to deal with finishes from the evaluation standpoint with only enough technical information to do so. The shooter who wants specific recipes for the older established procedures for doing his own finishing work should begin by reading Newell's excellent book.[87] The skeptical shooter who wants to evaluate new proprietary finishes must do what stockmakers do—test them on samples.

What do we expect a finish to do? If we look at the raw, light-colored, relatively soft and grainy surface of a finish-sanded stock we say: make the wood darker and bring out its figure and color, make its surface smoother and evener and harder. If we think about more intangible expectations, we ask for water-, oil-, and chemical-proof-ing, durability, flexibility, and easy repair. Moreover we want a surface texture quality that is pleasing in whatever way it is that makes silk more attractive than cellophane. We demand a lot from a few thousandths of an inch of chemical coating on the surface of a piece of wood. One approach is not to expect things of this little layer that it cannot do: it cannot withstand hard scratching or abrasion; it cannot bring out a beautiful grain or figure in a wood that doesn't have it.

The things a finish can do, and how well it can do them, may be better understood by reviewing the generally accepted steps in gunstock finishing. Regardless of what types of coatings are used, how many layers, how slow or fast they dry, or their cost in time and money, a good stock finish must in some way go through the processes outlined below or their equivalents.

PREPARATION OF THE SURFACE: Before any coating is applied the wood surface must be so smooth that no scratches will show through the transparent final finish. There need be no fear that the wood is too smooth to begin with since the bond between it and the finish is at the atomic level. It is chemical rather than mechanical. Excessive heat, however, during sanding may change the chemistry of the wood surface by "burnishing" and result in poor adhesion of the finish. Throughout the finishing work the surface must be kept protected from damage, dust, oil, or other contaminants. With the exception of some diffuse-porous woods, an agent must be used to *fill* the grain. This may be an inert filler powder applied as a paste and the excess removed after drying, or it may be the final finishing agent itself applied layer after layer and sanded down after each application to the level of the surface of the wood until the grain is filled. Whatever the wood or method used, the perfection of the appearance of the finish will depend more on the thoroughness of these preparations than on the type of finish used.

WATERPROOFING: The wood must be properly seasoned or kiln-dried to start with. Thereafter wood moisture content must be controlled throughout finishing by controlling shop humidity. Work begins with *whiskering*, raising the surface grain with water, followed by quick heat drying and removal of the excess wood, repeated until the grain no longer rises. The next step is *sealing*, the sufficient application of some moisture-resisting agent to all surfaces of the stock, both inside and out. The finish itself, as well as the sealer, should be as waterproof as possible. Waterproofing must be understood to be a relative term; all surface coatings are water-permeable to some extent.

COLORING: Coloring methods used before finishing include the application of very finely ground pigments or stains in solution, oxidizing chemicals, or flame. They all darken, lighten, or color the wood selectively, bringing out the figure if there is something to bring out. Colors used vary in the range of yellow, through brown and orange, to dull reds or even greens, grays, and blacks appropriate to the wood. Flame (the Siugi process) darkens the wood's own color. Many finishing agents have a slight yellowing effect. Some unstable finishes and coloring materials may be darkened or lightened by exposure to sunlight. It may be desirable to use bleaching agents to lighten some dark woods.

FINISHING: The choice of agent controls the durability and repairability of the finish. It must be applied in a way that will allow each layer to cure completely while building up a coat sufficiently thick to protect the wood of the stock and give it the luminosity which brings out the "depth" of the grain and figure of the wood. A thinner coat, however, will generally offer a better surface. Thick finishes scratch easily. Final finish thickness may vary between two and ten thousandths of an inch. Careful application and sanding between coats are necessary to prevent or correct uneven application, sags, bubbles, and other disasters.

POLISHING: Most commercial stocks are sold with a rather thick high-gloss finish. The cellophane-like reflecting quality of these surfaces can be reduced by polishing them with very fine abrasive materials such as pumice or rottenstone in some liquid medium. Depending on the agent used, the polished surface will tend to absorb instead of reflect light, feel softer, and look "richer."

Finishing is something of an art form involving a series of processes and materials that can be manipulated by the craftsman to produce a wide variety of effects. However the quality of the wood itself is the raw material. The finisher can change the color of the wood through a wide range, assure the smoothness of the surface by proper preparation, filling, and careful work, and control the luminosity and texture of the final finish by polishing. But his best efforts can only bring out the most the wood has to offer in grain and figure.

In selecting materials to be used, the choice is roughly between durable, high-performance materials and materials that lack these properties. Newell has pointed out in detail, in discussing different agents, the importance of using materials throughout the work that are chemically compatible with each other. This concept is also important in the repair or refinishing of old stocks where waxes and old finishing materials offer the opportunity to foul things up. The choice of efficient fillers, waterproofing agents, coloring agents, and finishes is wide enough to make it entirely unnecessary to use materials whose qualities are questionable.

Traditional filling agents include a variety of finely ground neutral substances mixed into a paste with some more or less adherent

Gunstock Finishes

binding agent. These fillers are, or can be, colored themselves and they may pick up too much or too little of a coloring agent applied to the stock after filling. The use of the finishing agent itself as a filler has several advantages: adhesion to the wood is superior, no coloring problem exists, and the final surface has greater depth and luminosity. Acceptable waterproofing agents include preparations containing silicon, varnish sealers, and various synthetics according to the reality of the claims made for them. As with filling, it's possible to kill another bird with the same stone by using the finishing preparation. Coloring agents of the pigment and dye types must be light-fast. Their penetration is highly variable in different woods as are the end results with given colors. They have a great deal to contribute to the beauty of the finish if they are skillfully used to enhance rather than kill the figure and contrast already existing in the wood. Colors that turn toward orange and red-browns are natural complementaries of the color of gun-bluing. Yellow-browns may have an unpleasing greenish tone against gun blue. Darker and neutral brown shades offer the best camouflage for guns to be used in blinds and can also conceal poor wood figure. The colors produced by flame are the most permanent and the most demanding of the operator's skill.

The ideal final finish material should combine the desired decorative qualities with hardness, toughness, and the all-important quality of flexibility. It should be as proof as possible against damage by light, heat, water, oil, and common chemicals and solvents. If it presents a high-gloss surface before polishing, it should be capable of being polished down to the desired degree of softer luster. The best grades of spar varnish and some synthetics offer these properties. Shellac (French polish), lacquer, and linseed oil (London oil), are all deficient in some respect. Their much admired surface sheen can be produced today by judicious polishing of good varnishes and synthetics without any sacrifice of other desirable qualities. In addition, these new materials offer the finisher the opportunity to combine some steps in the process, saving time and producing a less expensive finish of higher quality. The older, more time-consuming and laborious processes were only necessary to make the most out of the materials then available. The preparation of samples can prevent disappointment in regard to final color and surface texture.

Waxes and silicon cloth and spray preparations can offer additional surface protection but are not really necessary with a high quality finish. Waxes tend to dull and dampen the surface effect of really good finishes. Either may be artfully employed on guns offered for sale second-hand. The prospective buyer should look for their presence on used stocks. The real condition of a stock can only be judged after they are removed.

21
Checkering and Decoration Of Shotgun Stocks

This discussion of checkering is confined to those aspects that are of general interest to the shooter when purchasing or restocking a gun. Checkering layout is considered both from a practical standpoint and in relation to gun decoration. American shooters who are interested in trying the art of checkering for themselves are fortunate to have available the authoritative technical advice of Monty Kennedy and his collaborators.[88]

The durability of checkering is controlled by the quality of the wood, its finish after checkering, and by the proportions and spacing of the individual diamonds. Master checkerers prefer the best grades of *Juglans regia* because of their uniform density, hardness, and fine close grain—qualities essential for the clean cutting of small diamonds. Other woods are satisfactory for checkering to the extent that they meet these standards. Checkering in lighter, softer woods cannot be very finely spaced and is less resistant to wear. Coarse grained ring-porous woods, or soft spots in otherwise satisfactory blanks may result in irregular quality. Finishing can contribute a great deal to the durability of checkered areas but care must be exercised to preserve the sharpness of the diamonds. Newell stresses the importance of sealing the wood against moisture with whatever finishing technique is employed.[89]

Kennedy points out the relationship between durability and the architecture of the individual diamond. He prefers to cut with a 90 degree instead of an acute-angled tool in order to give the diamond a cross-sectional profile that is lower and structurally stronger. He advocates diamonds (as seen from above) proportioned 3½-1, a shape very similar to the 30-degree design recommended by Howe.[90] When diamonds of this proportion are arranged correctly on the

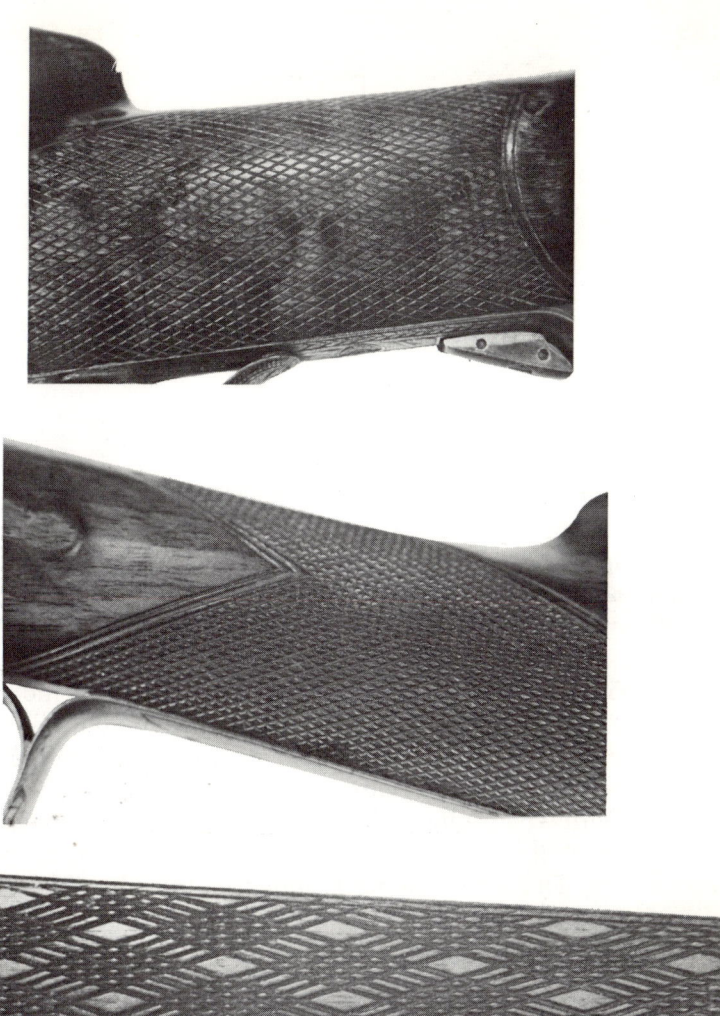

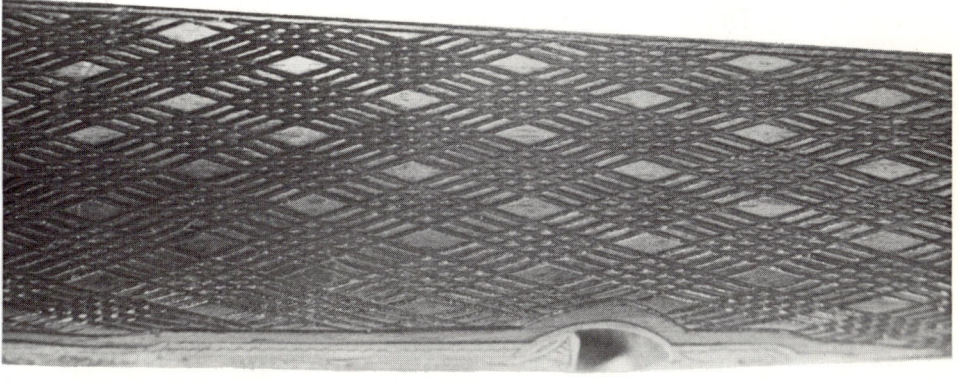

Fig. 37
Top, Checkering was first introduced about 1775 in a style like that on this early nineteenth century Purdey, now recognized as too flat and too blocky. (Abercrombie and Fitch)
Center, The evolution of checkering is shown in this Manton gun of about the same date: the diamonds are smaller, somewhat less blocky, and rounded at the upper edge. (Abercrombie and Fitch)
Bottom, One of the many possible styles of skip or "French" checkering which may or may not help the shooter hold his gun.

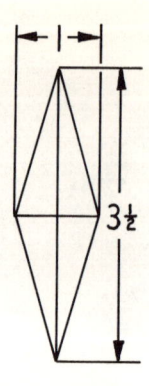

stock they seem to accelerate the flow of the lines of the gun and its stock. Although diamonds would be stronger as their proportions approached the square, the appearance of even 45 degree diamonds is unpleasantly blocky (Fig. 37, Top, Center). Very narrow diamonds are structurally weaker and their appearance is too linear.

Spacing of diamonds may vary from 16 to 32 lines per inch, with about 16 to 24 the common range. The closer the spacing in lines per inch, the finer and lower the diamonds, and the weaker and the more easily they are damaged or worn. Extremely fine spacing is usually restricted to otherwise expensive or "exhibition-grade" guns stocked with wood suitable for such fine work. Close spacing has the advantage of obscuring the figure of the wood less than does coarser checkering. Different spacing is sometimes used on the same stock

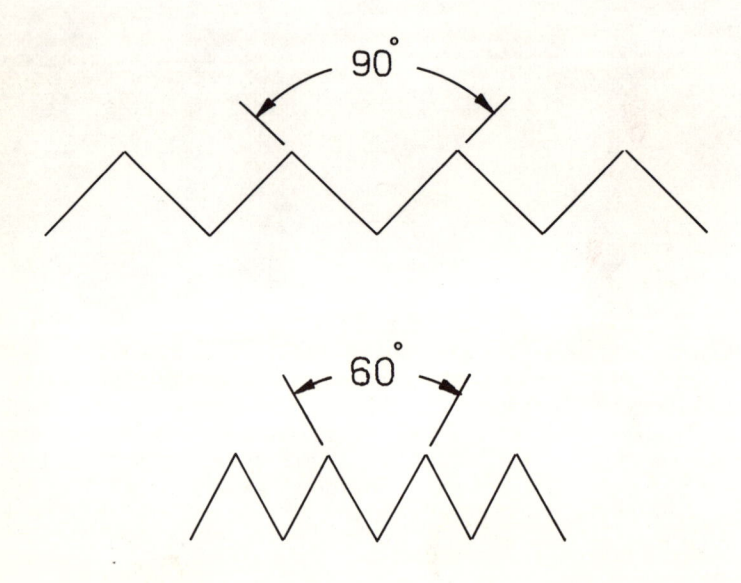

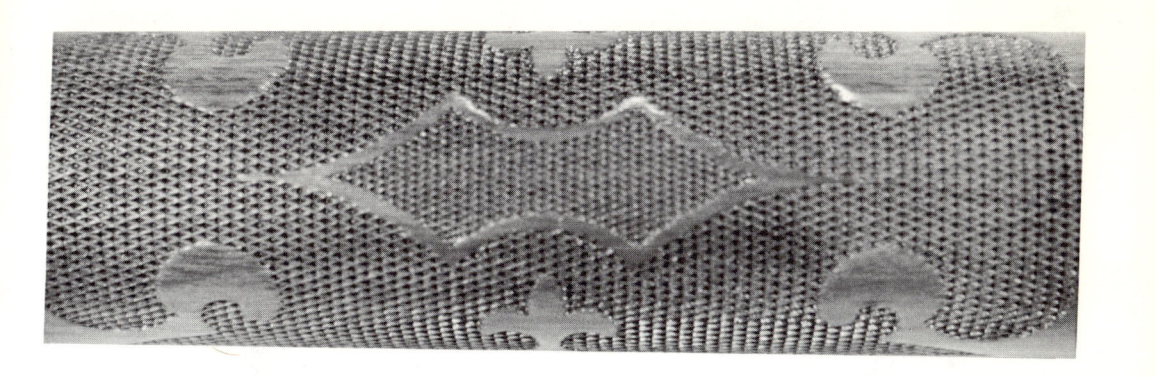

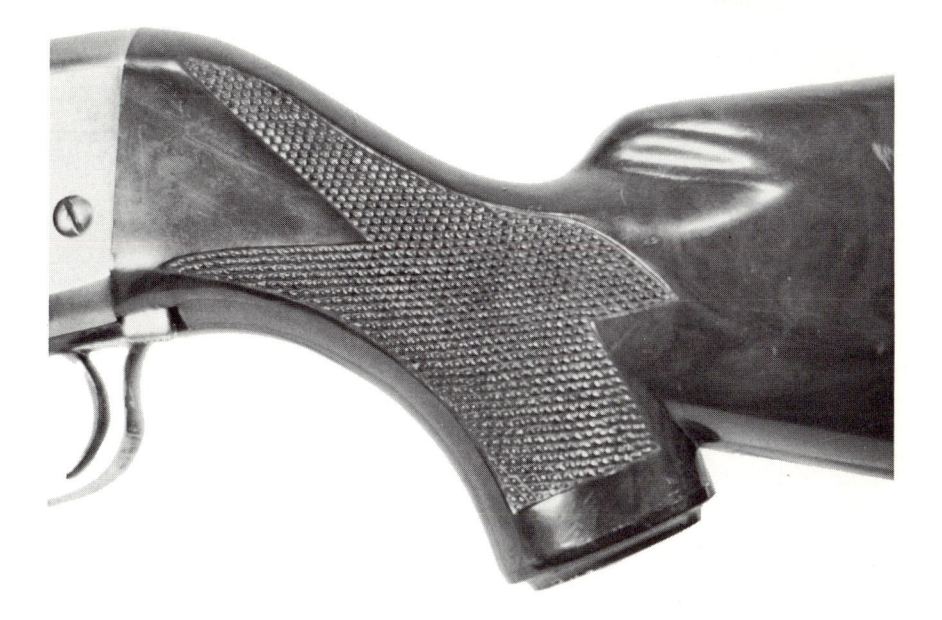

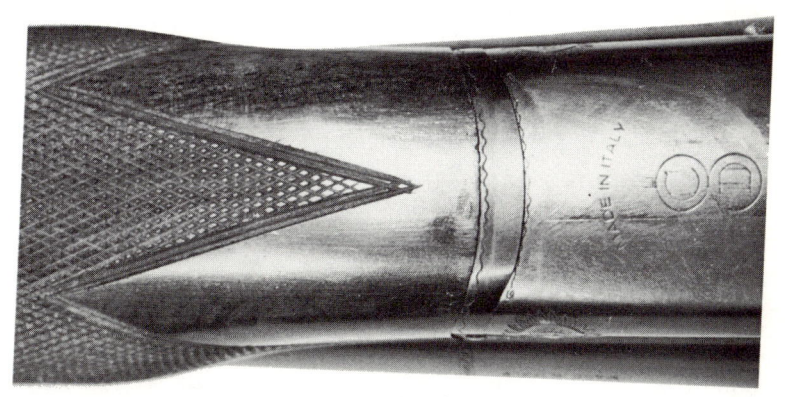

Fig. 38
Top, Machine checkering: the diamonds may be impressed into the wood (intaglio) instead of being elevated as in hand checkering. The surface is relatively smooth and catches dirt. Irregular crimping of the wood occurs at the edges.
Center, Molded checkering on a plastic stock: the crude raised diamonds have an unfamiliar shiny appearance avoided in properly finished hand checkered wood.
Bottom, Poor workmanship in hand checkering: irregularly flattened diamonds towards edges and angles, with runovers at borders.

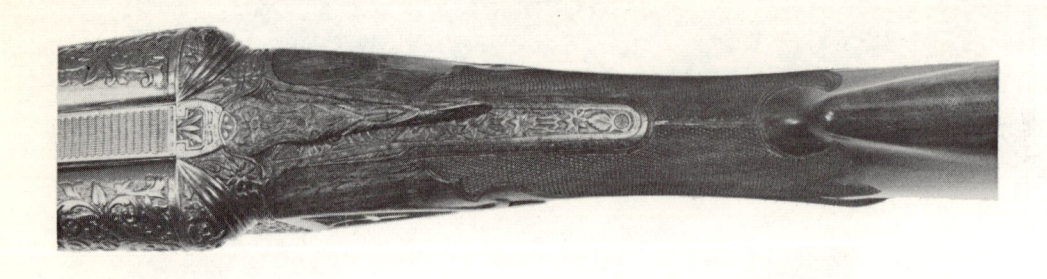

Fig. 39
Top, The elaborate checkering layout of this Parker is correct in principle because it covers the top of the grip and the area where the thumb comes to rest after releasing the safety. (Coll. Dr. Robert C. Snavely)
Bottom, The beginning of a layout style: the "point" checkering layout on this early-nineteenth-century Manton gun is entirely unrelated to the handsome curves of its locks or trigger guard. This design has continued to be popular because it is technically easy to execute. (Abercrombie and Fitch)

Checkering and Decoration of Shotgun Stocks

for its decorative effect. The overall appearance of checkering may be enhanced by matching its spacing to the type of gun and the style of the stock: wider spacing for larger heavier stocks and closer for lighter slimmer stocks.

Spacing should be kept within a range that makes the surface rough enough to help the shooter grip the gun—which, after all, is the practical purpose of checkering. This purpose is less efficiently served by the more flat-surfaced "English" style of checkering done with a tool which cuts right-angled dirt-catching grooves (Fig. 37, Top, Center). "French" or *skip* checkering also presents a smoother surface in proportion to the amount of skipping done (Fig. 37, Bottom). Machine checkering, at least at present, of either the intaglio or relief kind is largely decorative because it is too smooth to be useful (Fig. 38, Top). This fault is shared by the checkering on molded plastic stocks (Fig. 38, Center). Given a choice, the intelligent shotgunner of limited means could well forego this kind of mock-checkering for none at all.

By favoring simplified symmetrical stock shapes checkering, whether made by machine or hand, has indirectly done a disservice to stock fitting at the hand-hold areas. Machine checkering requires regular surfaces, and it is technically more difficult to checker irregularly rounded surfaces by hand. Even the shooter who has not tried checkering will easily recognize that the surface-area is greater over a convexity such as the Wundhammer swell. This increase in area means that the checkerer is obliged to carefully and tediously widen the spacing between his lines.[91] The time and level of skill required increases the cost of the work. The unfortunate result has been to limit the design of the grip areas of commercial shotgun stocks to simple shapes that are easy to checker by hand or machine instead of more subtle, rounded shapes that are easier to hold.

The details to judge checkering workmanship by are at the edge of the pattern: run-overs made by the checkering tools into borders and imperfect flattened diamonds where the tool has been lifted too soon (Fig. 38, Bottom). Too much has been made of checkering as an index of the general quality of a gun. Even the most perfect checkering is no guarantee of similar perfection in metal work. Quality in checkering unfortunately too often means quality of craftsmanship instead of quality of layout. Functionally and/or decoratively poor checkering layout is as common in higher priced guns as poor checkering workmanship in less expensive guns.

A functionally correct checkering layout should adequately cover both hand-hold areas. Particularly helpful is the type that extends around over the top of the grip, and onto the place where the thumb rests (Fig. 39, Top). On the fore-arm the checkering should extend

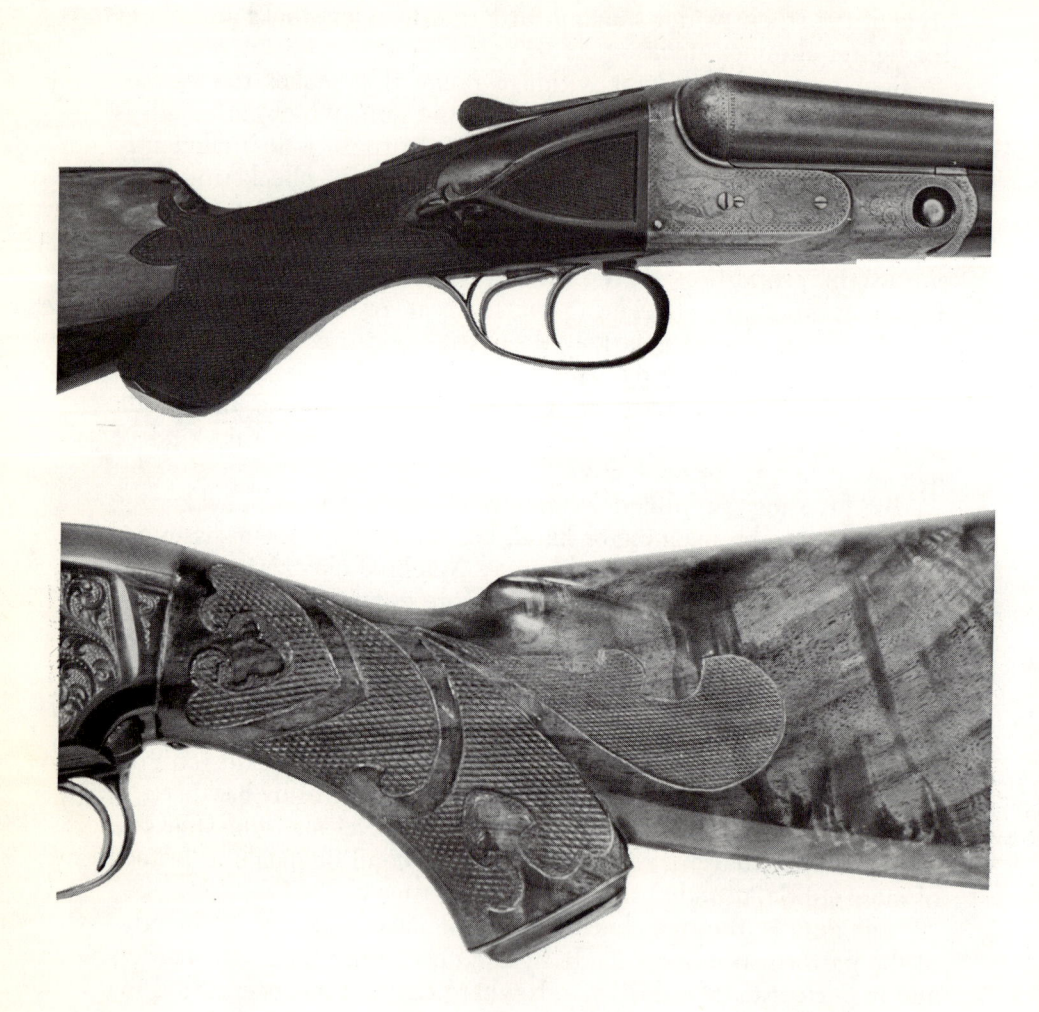

Fig. 40
Top, In contrast with the gun below, the rather elaborate checkering layout of Annie Oakley's Parker manages to be quite convincing. Its design elements are well related to each other and to the lines of the grip, simple enough not to clash with the unobtrusive engraving, and helped by the plainness of the wood. (Coll. Dr. Robert C. Snavely) **Bottom,** In the unimaginative "tradition" of American gun decoration, this repetitious **fleur de lis** layout interrupts the good lines of the Winchester Model 12 pistol grip and contradicts the figure of the wood where it extends uselessly back onto the body of the stock.

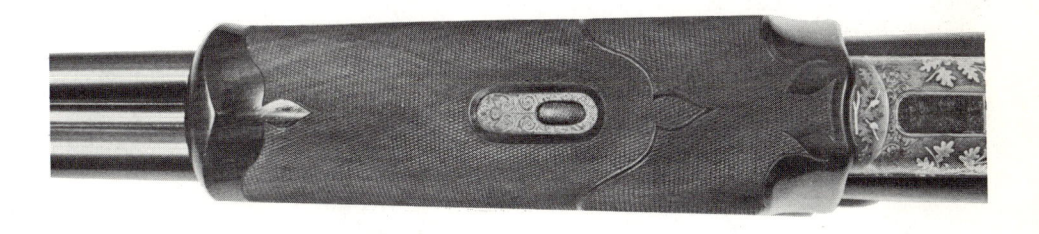

Checkering and Decoration of Shotgun Stocks 163

Fig. 41
The checkering layout of the fore-arm of this L. C. Smith superbly solves the difficult problem of its relationship to its Schnabel design and to its highly engraved and inlaid action by using broad areas and very simple lines on dark, dense, unfigured wood. (Coll. Dr. Robert C. Snavely)

high enough at the sides to present a rough surface to the thumb and fingertips as well as to the palm, and far enough forward along the bottom to do the same for these shooters who extend the forefinger there. On the other hand, that instinctive human horror of plain surfaces extends some checkering layouts onto places where no checkering is needed, such as the sides of the stock behind the grip (Fig. 40).

From the standpoint of appearance a good checkering layout must respect the fact that the shotgun stock is in two parts. The patterns should begin and end on either side of the action or receiver in a way that blends with the shape of the metal parts between. The lines of the stock should also be taken into consideration. The checkering layout should continue the flow of the gun and the stock without introducing contradictory or irrelevant lines or patterns (Fig. 39, Bottom). The spacing, layout, and borders of the checkering should be coordinated with any other form of decoration on the gun (Fig. 41).

The embellishment of the gun has traditionally consisted of engraving or precious metal inlays on its steel and the use of beautifully figured and colored woods for its stock, touched off with a monogrammed plaque. Although token engraving and suggestions of wood figure persist on guns in even the low price range, the increasing cost of fine decorative metal work and fine wood has probably been responsible for renewed interest in relatively less expensive forms of stock decoration: checkering layout, carving, and wood inlays.

Carving may be used for borders around checkering, or carved geometric or naturalistic patterns may be used in place of checkering. Representational or stylized decorative panels are sometimes carved on the off-side of the buttstock. Wood inlay of some complexity in color or design is occasionally used to enliven the appearance of very plain wood. Simpler inlays can be used to stabilize the effect of dramatically irregular figures in woods such as myrtle. Round, oval, diamond or shield-shaped silver or gold plaques or the owner's initials in metal are now customarily inlet on the lower edge of the buttstock or on the end of the pistol grip (Fig. 42). Before the introduction of the top-lever, they were set into the top of the grip just behind the action, a graceful location which could be used today on many repeating guns. Engraved with the owner's name or monogram, ovals look elegant and may discourage theft.

Guns are occasionally seen which combine nearly all possible decorative features. The results are ornate to florid (Fig. 43, Top). In decoration one good thing does not necessarily deserve another. Restraint is usually the key to good effect (Fig. 43, Bottom). The

Checkering and Decoration of Shotgun Stocks 165

Fig. 42
The owner's name or initials on the pistol grip cap or on the under edge of the buttstock midway between grip and toe can be handsome and may discourage larceny. (**Top,** Abercrombie and Fitch; **bottom,** Coll. Dr. Robert C. Snavely)

Fig. 43
Top, Ornate engraving and inlay work, an elaborate checkering layout, carved checkering borders and a carved plaque on the side of the stock, plus an open-sided recoil pad with a white "spacer" confuse the good lines of this gun so that the savant rightly called it, "Garbage!"
Bottom, Plain wood and an elegantly balanced checkering layout counter its metal inlays and engraving, keeping the good lines of this L. C. Smith clean so that it looks both simple and luxurious. (Coll. Dr. Robert C. Snavely)

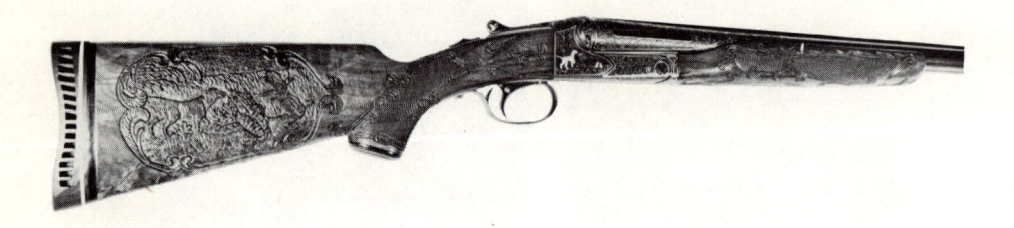

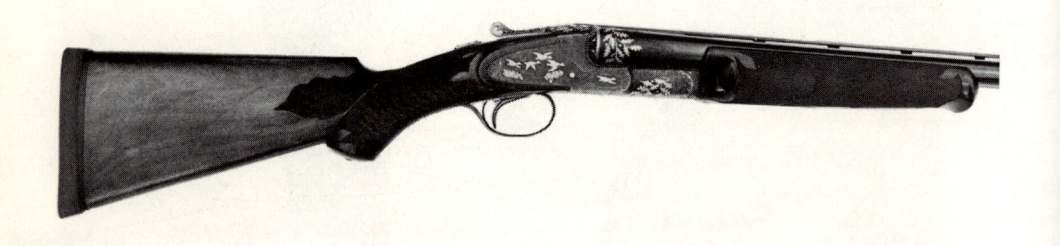

Checkering and Decoration of Shotgun Stocks 167

Fig. 44
Copycats. Contemporary gun engraving in a rut.

shooter with money enough to decorate a gun well should first make a general choice between emphasizing the metal or the wood. If he opts for prominent metal engraving or inlay work he should be content with a stock wood of subdued figure with discreet checkering (Fig. 8, Top). If he wishes the gun to be stocked with wood that is strikingly figured he might do best to choose a modest layout of very finely spaced checkering without complicated borders or do without checkering altogether (Fig. 28). Any engraving on such a gun should be unobtrusive. A compromise is the formula for British "best" gun decoration. Designed perhaps to give an appearance of richness commensurate with the gun's price, the fine-line rosette or scroll engraving covering the action and the darkly-finished pigment-figure wood with minimal checkering manage to look deceptively quiet.

Checkering layout has come to assume the principal role in decorating low- and medium-priced guns instead of acting as an adjunct to fine wood and engraving. It may end up with a bad reputation caused by flamboyant layouts intended to merchandise guns (Fig. 38, Top). Of the lesser forms of gun decoration, inlay work may be at its best when employed to enliven a monotonous wood under the rules previously described. Carving is a special case since any amount of it cannot help dominating the gun's appearance. The right recipe for its use would seem to be to suppress every other form of decoration. The problem is to find carvers who are both artist-designers and craftsmen. In no other field of gun decoration is there reason to complain about the quality of workmanship as well as design. Checkering and engraving skills of the highest order are available. Their best work, however, still dismally echoes the taste of past generations of artist-designers in firearms (Fig. 44). There is an opportunity for some shotgun-loving Maecenas to commission original work from artist-craftsmen in wood and metal from outside the chauvinistic confines of the firearms industry who might succeed in applying the possibilities of modern design to present-day gun decoration.

Notes

1. Frank Forester (H. W. Herbert), *The Complete Manual For Young Sportsmen* (New York: George E. Woodward, 1873), p. 44.
2. Willi Barthold, *Jagdwaffenkunde* (Suhl: VEB Ernst Thälmann-Werk, 1964), p. 219.
3. These guns were all of the "game gun" type for their period, with relatively short barrels, small gauge, and light weight. There was no evidence that their stocks were not original. Six of the guns were from the collection of the Winchester Museum, New Haven, Conn., and four from that of the Arms and Armor Dept. of the Metropolitan Museum of Art, N.Y., N.Y. Each institution provided information dating their manufacture.
4. Bob Nichols, *Skeet and How to Shoot It* (New York: Greenberg, 1939), p. 69.
5. Major Sir Gerald Burrard, *The Modern Shotgun* 2 vols. (New York: A. S. Barnes and Co., 1961), III, p. 242.
6. Colonel Charles Askins, *The Shotgunner's Book* (Harrisburg, Pa.: The Stackpole Co., 1958), p. 45.
7. Robert Churchill, *Churchill's Shotgun Book* (New York: Alfred A. Knopf, 1955), p. 107.
8. Fred Etchen, *How to be an Expert at Shotgun Shooting* (Greenwich, Conn.: Fawcett Publications, Inc., 1960), p. 72.
9. Personal communication.
10. Etchen, *Shotgun Shooting*, p. 71.
11. Churchill, *Shotgun Book*, p. 110.
12. Churchill, *Shotgun Book*, p. 47.
13. Townsend Whelen, *Small Arms Design and Ballistics* 2 vols. (Georgetown, S.C.: Small Arms Technical Publishing Co., 1945), II, p. 53.
14. Burrard, *Modern Shotgun*, III, pp. 237-8.
15. Etchen, *Shotgun Shooting*, p. 72.
16. Arthur Hearn, *Shooting and Gunfitting* (London: Herbert Jenkins, Ltd, n.d.), p. 29.
17. W. W. Greener, *The Gun and Its Development*, 9th ed. (New York: Bonanza Books, n.d.), p. 423.
18. Burrard, *Modern Shotgun*, I, p. 135.
19. Askins, *Shotgunner's Book*, p. 50.
20. Churchill, *Shotgun Book*, pp. 105-6.
21. Greener, *The Gun*, p. 423.
22. Elmer Keith, *Shotguns by Keith* (Harrisburg, Pa.: The Stackpole Co., 1961), p. 157.
23. Bob Nichols, *The Shotgunner* (New York: G. P. Putnam's Sons, 1949), p. 174.
24. Jack O'Connor, *Complete Book of Rifles and Shotguns* (New York: Outdoor Life, Harper and Bros., 1961), p. 414.

25. Francis E. Sell, *The American Shotgunner* (Harrisburg, Pa.: The Stackpole Co., 1962), p. 101.
26. Sir Ralph F. Payne-Gallwey, Bart., *High Pheasants in Theory and Practice* (London: Longmans, Green, and Co., 1913), pp. 6–8.
27. Hearn, *Gunfitting*, p. 29.
28. Percy Stanbury and G. L. Carlisle, *Shotgun Marksmanship* (New York: A. S. Barnes and Co., 1962), pp. 57–8.
29. Barthold, *Jagdwaffen*, p. 220.
30. Greener, *The Gun*, p. 423.
31. Francis E. Sell, "Low Cost Custom Doubles," *Gun Digest,* 20th ed. (1966), p. 169.
32. Keith, *Shotguns,* p. 145.
33. Julian S. Hatcher, *Hatcher's Notebook* (Harrisburg, Pa.: The Stackpole Co., 1966), p. 293.
34. Lt. Col. P. Hawker, *Instructions to Young Sportsmen in All that Relates to Guns and Shooting,* 4th ed. (London: Longman, Hurst, Rees, Orme, Brown, and Green, 1825), pp. 27–8.
35. Churchill, *Shotgun Book,* pp. 34–5.
36. Burrard, *Modern Shotgun,* I, p. 137.
37. Gough Thomas, *Shotguns and Cartridges* (London: Percival Marshall and Co., 1963), pp. 91–3.
38. Barthold, *Jagdwaffen,* p. 219.
39. Etchen, *Shotgun Shooting,* p. 72.
40. Greener, *The Gun,* pp. 423–5.
41. Keith, *Shotguns,* pp. 137–8.
42. Burrard, *Modern Shotguns,* I, pp. 131–4.
43. Thomas, *Shotguns and Cartridges,* pp. 85–93.
44. Gough Thomas (G. T. Garwood), *Gough Thomas's Gun Book* (London: Adam and Charles Black, 1969), pp. 37–9.
45. Nichols, *Shotgunner,* pp. 134–5.
46. Charles Lancaster, *The Art of Shooting,* 11th ed. (London: Charles Lancaster and Co., 1945), p. 21.
47. Rolla B. Boughan, *Shotgun Ballistics for Hunters* (New York: A. S. Barnes and Co., London: Thomas Yoseloff, Ltd., 1965), pp. 90–109.
48. Clair F. Rees, "Pick a Goose Gun," *Shooting Times,* Vol. 10, No. 7 (July 1969), p. 26.
49. Burrard, *Modern Shotgun,* I, pp. 221–8.
50. Whelen, *Design and Ballistics,* pp. 50–72.
51. Thomas, *Gun Book,* pp. 172–5.
52. Gough Thomas, "A Bad Defect and Its Cure," *Shooting Times and Country Magazine,* No. 4507 (March 22, 1969), p. 449.
53. Francis E. Sell, *Sure-Hit Shotgun Ways* (Harrisburg, Pa.: The Stackpole Press, 1967), pp. 111–2.
54. Nichols, *Shotgunner,* p. 108.
55. Hugh S. Gladstone, *Record Bags and Shooting Records* (London: H. F. and G. Witherby, 1922), p. 123.
56. Nichols, *Shotgunner,* p. 115.
57. James Virgil Howe, *The Modern Gunsmith,* 2 vols. (New York: Funk and Wagnalls Co., 1954), I, p. 117.
58. Lloyd Carlson, "Handicapped Shooters," *Guns and Ammo,* Vol. 13, No. 7 (July 1969), p. 55.
59. G. H. Teasdale-Buckell, *The Complete Shot,* 5th ed. (London: Methuen and Co., 1924), p. 96.

Notes

60. Churchill, *Shotgun Book,* pp. 150–1.
61. James J. Gibson, *The Perception of the Visual World* (Boston: Houghton Mifflin Co., 1950), p. 29.
62. Burrard, *Modern Shotgun,* III, pp. 245–55.
63. Nichols, *Shotgunner,* pp. 94–114.
64. Nichols, *Shotgunner,* p. 112.
65. Nichols, *Shotgunner,* p. 156.
66. Nichols, *Shotgunner,* pp. 104–5.
67. Boughan, *Shotgun Ballistics,* pp. 71–8.
68. Burrard, *Modern Shotgun,* III, pp. 80, 101–2.
69. Dr. George G. Oberfell and Charles E. Thompson, *The Mysteries of Shotgun Patterns* (Stillwater, Okla.: Oklahoma State University Press, 1960), p. 143.
70. Burrard, *Modern Shooter,* p. 102.
71. Oberfell and Thompson, *Shotgun Patterns,* pp. 143–6.
72. Wallace Labisky, "Wind and The Shot Charge," *Shooting Times,* Vol. 9, No. 12 (December 1968), p. 44.
73. Burrard, *Modern Shotgun,* II, pp. 115–59.
74. Oberfell and Thompson, *Shotgun Patterns.*
75. Robert J. Robel, "Custom Made Shooting for Custom Made Guns," *The American Rifleman.* Vol. 116, No. 11 (November 1968), pp. 43–5.
76. Burrard, *Modern Shotgun,* III, p. 241.
77. This general concept is certainly not an original one. Lawrence B. Smith in his *Shotgun Psychology* (New York: Charles Scribner's Sons, 1938), pp. 22–4, describes and illustrates a crude "try-stock." The new stock prepared from it required considerable modification after it left the stockmaker's hands because the fit of the "try-stock" had not been perfected. The author wishes to emphasize the importance of prolonged testing by shooting and modification of the try-stock *before* any attempt is made to copy it.
78. Howe, *Modern Gunsmith.*
79. David A. Webb, "Adhesives—A Sticky Problem for Gunsmiths," *The American Rifleman,* Vol. 117, No. 7 (July 1969), pp. 44–6.
80. *Wood Handbook,* U.S. Dept. of Agriculture Handbook No. 72, 1955.
81. Personal Communication.
82. H. B. Brown, A. J. Parshin, and C. C. Forsaith, *Textbook of Wood Technology,* 2 vols. (New York: McGraw-Hill Book Co., 1949–52).
83. Alexander L. Howard, *A Manual of the Timbers of the World* (London: Macmillan and Co., 1920).
84. Monty Kennedy, *Checkering and Carving of Gunstocks* (Harrisburg, Pa.: The Stackpole Co., 1962), pp. 94–6.
85. Howe, *Modern Gunsmith,* I, p. 87.
86. Clyde Baker, *Modern Gunsmithing* (Plantersville, S.C.: Small Arms Technical Publishing Co., 1933), p. 86.
87. Ronald A. Newell, *Gunstock Finishing and Care* (Harrisburg, Pa.: The Stackpole Co., 1966).
88. Kennedy, *Checkering.*
89. Newell, *Gunstock Finishing,* pp. 56–9, 327–32.
90. Howe, *Modern Gunsmith,* I, pp. 179–97.
91. Kennedy, *Checkering,* p. 57.

Index

Anson fore-end latch, 45

Balance, shotgun, 82–88; point of, 63
Ballistics, shotgun, 82–88
Bend, 22
Body of the stock, 59–60
Bridge-gap, 79
Bump, 21
Butt, 21–26; chamfered, 23; -plate, 23–26

Carving, stock, 64, 168
Cast, 30–33
    -at-heel, 30
    -at-toe, 30
    measuring for, 33
    -off, 30
    -on, 33
Checkering, 156–161
    layout, 161, 164, 168
    proportions of, 156
    quality of, 161
    spacing, 158–161
Cheekpiece, 55–58
    Bavarian, 56
    pancake, 55
    roll-over, 58
    saddle, 55
Comb, 46–54, 89–92, 105–106
    fitting, 89–92, 105–106
    Greener Rational, 51
    level, 50–51
    line-of-sight, 51–54
    Monte-Carlo, 46–47, 51
    roll-over, 58, 108
    Schweinsrücken, 51
    temporary sight and, 92
    -to-eye distance, 50

Decoration, gun, 164, 168
Design, shotgun stock, 95–104
    for over-and-under guns, 102
    for repeating guns, 99–100
    for side-by-side guns, 16–99
    for sliding breech guns, 99–100
    gun type and, 96
    rifle stock and, 102–103
    try-stock in, 115–125
Drop-at-comb, 46–52
Drop-at-heel, 22, 46–52

Engraving, gun, 164, 168
Eye-catcher notch, 78

Figure, wood, 133–144
    birdseye, 139, 148
    blister, 139
    broken stripe, 139
    burl (burr), 144
    crotch, 139, 143
    curly, 138, 139
    fiddleback, 139, 142
    flat-(slab-)sawed, 139, 140
    pigment, 144
    quarter-sawed, 139, 140
    quilted, 116, 139
    ray-fleck, 139
    ribbon, 139
    silver grain, 139
    stripe, 139
    stump, 103, 133, 139
Finish, gunstock, 152–155
    agents, 155
    burnishing during, 153
    color, 153–154, 155
    of checkering, 156
    polishing, 154
    silicon, 155
    Siugi process, 147, 154
    wax, 155
    whiskering, 153
Fitting, stock, 17–60, 89–92, 105–125
    by remodeling, 108–109, 113–114
    by try-gun, 106–108
    by try stock, 109–113
    procedure in, 115–125
Flyers, 82
Fore-arm, 40
Fore-end, 40–45
    beavertail, 40

clip-on, 43
Colley, 40
handle, 40
Schnabel, 42, 99
shell, 40
splinter, 40

Grip, 34–39
  cap, 35, 165
  Etchen, 34
  pistol, 34
  straight, 35–36
  taper, 36
  thumb-hole, 39, 102

Heel, 21

Inlay, wood, 164, 168

Length: of pull, 17; of stock, 17–20
Line-of-sight, 49; comb, 47–48

Manton guns, 17–18, 53
Master eye, 32, 76–78

Pattern, shot, 82–87
  air density and, 83
  grouping of, 84
  quality of, 90–91
  sighting-in and, 91–92
Permissible error of aim: at the comb, 86–87; at the target, 83–84
Pitch, 27–29
Plaque, initialed, 164

Recoil, 65–68
  cast and, 32, 66
  drop-at-heel and, 22–23, 66
  flip, 67
  jump, 65
  line-of-sight and, 53
  nomograph, 65
  pads, 26
  vibration, 67
Regulation, barrel
  cartridges and, 67–68
  recoil and, 65–68
  testing for, 89–91
Ribs, 78–81: Churchill, 80

Shooters
  ambidextrous, 69–70
  handicapped, 69–74
  one-armed, 73
Shot
  bore and ammunition, 82–87
  effective, 82
  stringing, 86

trajectory, 85
wind and, 85
Side-lock, 99
Sight, shotgun, 75–81
  Bev-L-Blok, 79
  Glow Worm, 80–81
  Greener Monopeian, 70, 78
  Hogan-Howe, 70, 78
  Nydar, 81
  offset, 70, 78
  -plane (single, double), 78–79
  Raybar, 80–81
  Singlepoint, 81
  temporary, 90
Sighting-in, 89–92
Sliding breech, 99–101
Small, 34
Spacers, 26
Stand, 27
Stock, shotgun
  anti-recoil, 65
  cross-over, 70
  decoration of, 156–168
  design of, 95–100
  dog-leg, 70
  experimental, 115–125
  finishes, 152–155
  fitting, 17–60, 89–92, 105–125
  for children, 20
  gooseneck, 70
  Greener Rational, 51
  layout, 131–135
  line-of-sight, 51–54
  Monte-Carlo, 46–47, 51
  plastic, 134
  remodeling, 108–109, 113–114
  Rigby one-arm, 65
  roach-bellied, 60
  Schweinsrücken, 51
  special, 69–74
Straight, 22

Toe, 21
Try-gun, 106–108
Try-stock, 109–113, 115–125

Undercut, 59–60

Vision: binocular, 76; gradient of clarity of, 75

Wood, gunstock, 129–151
  drying, 130
  figure in, 133–144
  oil and, 130–131
  physical properties, 129–134
  sawing, 136, 139

Index

varieties of, 144–151
Wood, structure of
  annual rings, 134
  diffuse-porous, 134, 148
  heartwood, 144
  medullary rays, 134
  ring-porous, 134–138
  sapwood, 144
  spring, 134, 138
  summer, 134, 138,
Wood, varieties of
  African walnut, 151
  apple, 145
  ash, 130, 145, 146
  beech, 130, 145
  birch, 130, 145
  cherry, 130, 145
  Claro walnut, 151
  lacewood, 64, 146
  laminated, 146
  madrone, 146
  mahogany, 145, 146
  maple, 64, 130–131, 145, 146–147
  mesquite, 147
  myrtle, 145, 147–150
  padouk, 150
  Papapsco, 146
  Patapsco, 146
  pecan, 145
  persimmon, 145, 150
  rosewood, 150
  sycamore, 64, 130, 139, 145
  tigerwood, 151
  vermilion, 150
  walnut, 130, 145, 150–151, 156
  zebra, 151
Wundhammer swell, 39, 122–123